Coping
with Grief

FIFTH EDITION

Mal McKissock and
Dianne McKissock

Foreword by Hon. Dame Marie Bashir AD CVO

ABC
Books

The ABC 'Wave' device is a trademark of the
Australian Broadcasting Corporation and is used
under licence by HarperCollinsPublishers Australia.

First published in Australia in 1988
This edition published in 2018
by HarperCollins*Publishers* Australia Pty Limited
ABN 36 009 913 517
harpercollins.com.au

HarperCollins*Publishers*
Level 13, 201 Elizabeth Street, Sydney, NSW 2000, Australia
Unit D1, 63 Apollo Drive, Rosedale, Auckland 0632, New Zealand
A 53, Sector 57, Noida, UP, India
1 London Bridge Street, London, SE1 9GF, United Kingdom
Bay Adelaide Centre, East Tower, 22 Adelaide Street West, 41st Floor,
    Toronto, Ontario, M5H 4E3
195 Broadway, New York, NY 10007, USA

A catalogue record for this book is available from the National Library of Australia

ISBN 978 0 7333 3957 8 (pbk)
ISBN 978 1 4607 1059 3 (ebook)

Cover design by HarperCollins Design Studio
Cover image by Shutterstock.com
Typeset in 12/16pt Aldine 401 BT by HarperCollins Design Studio
Printed and bound in Australia by McPherson's Printing Group
The papers used by HarperCollins in the manufacture of this book are a natural,
recyclable product made from wood grown in sustainable plantation forests.
The fibre source and manufacturing processes meet recognised international
environmental standards, and carry certification.

We dedicate this book to people everywhere who have experienced, or are currently experiencing, the pain of grief. We hope the words in this book make you feel understood.

Our thoughts are also with those who provide compassionate care — folk prepared to walk symbolically alongside bereaved people until the path ahead feels survivable.

Contents

Foreword

by Hon. Dame Marie Bashir AD CVO

There can be no doubt that the death of an individual, whether expected or without any warning, can be a unique catastrophe in the life of an individual, a family or even a community. Moreover, coping with the grief process may present the greatest of emotional and other personal challenges ever to be confronted.

The authors of this volume, *Coping with Grief* — Mal McKissock and Dianne McKissock — both sensitively attuned to this experience of ultimate loss, have been able to identify ways in which to meet this challenge in the most constructive manner. Ever empathic, they have made this wisdom and its applicability available to anyone who would wish to apply such knowledge in their own experience of loss and grief, or that of a dear relative or friend.

At the outset their words endorse the uniqueness of the individual in mourning, by their forthright statement 'There is no right or wrong way to grieve.'

Indeed, they provide further support to the individual, whatever their presentation, following bereavement. 'We all grieve as we have lived... emotionally expressive people might become more expressive, those who don't show feelings openly may appear even more contained'; and further, '...when an expressive person is forced to contain emotion, they may later experience physical symptoms or even illness as a result'.

As the authors have noted, unresolved grief may, much later, contribute to vulnerability, to either physical or psychological illness, or indeed to both; and that platitudinous remarks from caregivers — no matter how well intentioned — are rarely of value. This became evident, resulting in a new body of research and study, in the condition known as 'post-traumatic stress disorder'.

Characteristics of the grieving process over several days following bereavement are given openly, and in some instances with valuable anecdotes from the experience of a grieving individual.

A special mention is made of the significance for the grieving individual of anniversaries and special dates, and the wisdom of having a trusted and empathic individual available — even on 'standby' — in case the understandable flood of emotions becomes overwhelming. Such a valued individual can also validate the right — the normality — of the bereaved to experience such a powerful sense of emotional loss, dispelling guilt if anger or abandonment is felt.

Wisdom is also offered in pointing out which questions and which topics may be helpful when raised with the bereaved person, and which may have the reverse effect. In addition, the value of retention of social connection is emphasised, despite the presence at times of a sense of personal guilt that one does not remain submerged in the darker environment of overwhelming loss.

Many aspects of 'self-help' and simple lifestyle inclusions, such as adequate sleep and nutritious food and a normal physical momentum, are noted, and sensitive acknowledgement of the role of 'memorialisation' — whether spiritual (according to the individual's affiliation) or physical, such as a tombstone or even social-media mention.

This sensitively written volume provides a truly comprehensive overview of all aspects of 'coping with grief', and will provide support to innumerable individuals and groups in the years ahead.

Professor the Honourable
Dame Marie Bashir AD CVO

Introduction

Loss

The experience of grief in response to loss is known to all human beings regardless of age, gender, creed or culture. Extremes of grief tend to be experienced when we lose a close and meaningful relationship through divorce, separation, estrangement or death. We may also grieve the loss of a limb, ability, appearance, country, home, meaningful occupation, trust or lifestyle.

Responses to all losses have many characteristics in common, but it is generally agreed that death is the most significant loss for most of us, perhaps because of its finality and confrontation with our own finiteness.

Whatever the cause of loss, there is little benefit in making comparisons of 'worseness'. Grief is a subjective experience and most of us feel little benefit in being told there is someone worse off than ourselves. We can only feel our own pain. For example, if I have a toothache or migraine, I am unlikely to find comfort in being told that someone else has a worse one.

While this book focuses on grief following bereavement, people grieving other losses may be able to identify with many of the reactions and responses described.

In our society, people tend to be intolerant of strong reactions to pain. After a very short time, even after a sudden or traumatic death, others may use clichés to placate feelings and say things like 'buck up', 'think of the kids', 'every cloud has a silver lining', 'it's God's will', 'he/she is in a better place', 'they wouldn't want you to be upset', 'you're young enough — you can have another baby', 'you can get married again…'. While usually expressed from concern and a genuine belief that getting upset is bad for you, platitudes and clichés are designed, consciously or unconsciously, to prevent feelings being expressed.

If you do show distress openly, you may be described (or describe yourself) as 'breaking down', 'falling apart', 'cracking up' or 'not coping'. All of these terms are derogatory and patronising, and demonstrate a lack of understanding of the nature and process of grief. Conversely, if you demonstrate stoical restraint when someone you love has died you are likely to be described as 'brave', 'strong', 'courageous', 'holding yourself together' or 'coping well'. All of these expressions are examples of how language is used to prevent or control expression of feelings.

There is no right or wrong way to grieve

We all grieve as we have lived. For example, emotionally expressive people might become more expressive, those who don't show feelings openly may appear even more contained. Problems may occur when others try to force us to behave in ways that are comfortable for them, and not expressions of who we are. For example, when an expressive person is forced to contain emotion, they may later experience physical symptoms or even illness as a result.

This book gives an outline of the grieving process and some of the reactions that occur when we are bereaved, along with suggestions for managing grief so that unnecessary suffering is minimised. It is suitable for those supporting bereaved people, as well as for anyone who is grieving the death of someone they love.

Some of the ideas included may seem strange at first to those who have not experienced significant loss.

However, they are based on many years of experience in working with bereaved people, and on personal experience of grief. They have the capacity to increase compassionate understanding, enhance relationships, and facilitate the bereaved person's ability to learn how to live with grief.

The language used in this book, whether sounding personal or more general, is meant to include us all. As mentioned earlier, grief is a great leveller, a common, human experience.

There are several basic principles to remember:

- It is normal and healthy to feel and express intense and painful emotions when grieving a significant loss.
- Expressions of grief help bereaved people learn how to live with loss.
- A bereaved person may experience a wide range of feelings — shock, sadness, anger, guilt, despair, as well as relief, hope and acceptance.
- Bereaved people do *not* grieve in stages — grief is not linear, but is chaotic — an 'all over the shop' experience.
- Painful feelings decrease in intensity over time if the bereaved person receives the kind of compassionate support that is right for them. If intensity does not abate after a significant

period of time, that may be an indication that professional help may be required.

- A total absence of observable grief may also be an indication of the need for professional help — an emotional 'check-up'.
- Bereaved people who have not been helped to express grief in ways that are right for them are likely to be more vulnerable to physical and psychological illness in the long term.

Normal responses of care-givers

Before discussing common reactions of bereaved people, let's briefly talk about some common reactions of those in a supportive or caretaking role. It is 'normal', sensitive and empathic to feel helpless, to be filled with longing to find something to do or say that will make the bereaved person feel better. It is at this point of helplessness that many carers are likely to use platitudes such as 'it's just a matter of time', words which are never found to be helpful to anyone. It is appropriate to feel pain when someone we love dies, and all that most of us need at these times is for a caring person to have the courage to stay and listen to how much it hurts, resisting any temptation to try to fix things, to make 'it' all better.

Despite the comment above about 'time' being used in a patronising way, time *is* an important aspect of grief.

Initially,
Time
   ...stands still
      ...weighs heavily
         ...passes
            ...heals.

This doesn't refer to the clichés mentioned earlier, but rather to a subjective, internal process — someone else's words applied externally like a band aid cannot create healing. The process has to be experienced by each bereaved person in their own way.

Let's look for a moment at some of the other time factors associated with bereavement.

Time factors associated with bereavement

The first day

When the death is sudden or traumatic, there is usually a sense of shock and a general feeling of numbness. This reaction is both emotional and physical — emotional to protect us from painful knowledge, and physical to stimulate the necessary bodily chemicals which help us to survive in intense situations.

Associated with numbness may be behaviour that appears to be denial. For example, we may say something like 'No, it can't be true' or 'It must be a mistake'. This defensive reaction is an attempt to push reality away, to cushion the blow, to protect ourselves from trauma. Initial reactions may last from several minutes to hours, or even days, and there may be little other expression of feelings, and not much clear thinking. It is helpful to have an understanding person close by at this time, someone who is not afraid of strong feelings when they emerge, someone who is able to act in a supportive role, making sure that the environment is safe, and that no one interferes inappropriately or unhelpfully.

Numbness may give way to overwhelming feelings that may be expressed in crying, screaming, yelling, kicking or withdrawing. Self-control is not helpful, nor are platitudes from others like 'buck up and think of the kids'. Children will do better in the long term if we as adults model healthy ways to grieve, and a caring support person can also help by explaining that 'It may be a bit scary to see/hear your parents expressing strong feelings, but everything will be alright. We will all take care of each other'.

Many people are offered drugs at this time, sometimes within hours of a death, but they are usually not helpful. Numbness, disbelief, shock, confusion, sadness, anger, guilt, fear, loss of appetite, nausea, restlessness, agitation and sleeplessness are all distressing but normal reactions and will be discussed further as we go. Tempting as it may be to dull the pain of grief, alcohol and other drugs tend to interfere with or delay a necessary process.

The third day

This seems to be another significant time for bereaved people. Reality is beginning to sink in in small bursts, numbness may be starting to wear off, and pain increasing. Days and nights may have passed in a blur, and it may still be difficult to sustain belief that this event has really happened. Some people may wish it was them who had died. In the midst of this distress and confusion, a funeral may have to be arranged. It is often helpful to slow this process down, to postpone the funeral until the death seems more real and clear thinking is more possible.

It is not necessary to have a funeral within three days, despite some pressure that may be exerted by funeral directors or family members. Contrary to popular belief, getting the funeral over with does not speed up the grieving process, and certainly does not mean bereaved people can now 'put it all behind them and get on with life'. A funeral after the third day — perhaps a week or even ten days later — may allow the family time to prepare a funeral that is a meaningful expression of the life of the person who died, and a more satisfying experience for everyone involved.

One of the pressures that influence the timing of a funeral in Australia is that most people are only allowed three days' compassionate leave from their work situation when a close relative dies.

The seventh day

In the beginning, relatives and friends converge from far and wide to pay their respects and offer love and consolation.

Seven days later they have all but disappeared as they return to the everyday demands of their own lives. After the adrenalin rush of the death and funeral, bereaved people often feel deserted and overwhelmed with loneliness. For many, sunset on day seven may mark a time when they feel at their worst. Being alone with increasing awareness of the reality of death may produce feelings of despair, fears of 'am I going mad?' or 'how will I ever be able to survive?'. These fears may descend like a black cloud, without warning, leaving the bereaved person desolate, desperate, and crying out for relief. At this time it can be tempting to seek solace in alcohol or other drugs — one of the few things that can provide an illusion of control.

Four to six weeks later

This is the time people tend to say 'it's getting worse,

it's not getting any better, I'm going downhill'. An adult child may phone a relative, friend or professional and say a version of 'I'm really worried about Mum. Dad died five weeks ago and at the time she was really brave, she coped really well, much better than we thought she would, but now she's going downhill, not eating very much, not sleeping and she's crying a lot more than she did when it happened. I just don't know what to do'.

It is important for any helper to first listen to the 'child's' (or supporter's) concern, acknowledge how difficult it might be to see what is happening to Mum. Then ask about Dad's death and generally encourage her/him to talk about it. Later, reassure him/her that what is happening to Mum is to be expected — it is not that pain and despair are getting worse, simply that the body's protective devices are wearing off. Feelings that have been there all along are coming to the surface and are a good sign, even if distressing to witness.

What Mum needs now is to be with someone who will let her express her feelings without criticism, not someone who will force feed her and then knock her out with sedatives. She needs to be able to talk about her experiences over and over again until she feels in control of her grief, not 'it' in control of her.

The first year

In the first year many people describe grief as 'coming in waves', often at the most unexpected times and in the most unexpected places. For instance, the bereaved person may be cleaning their teeth and not thinking about anything in particular, when all of a sudden they are overwhelmed by despair. Shopping in the supermarket is another common place to experience intense grief. Reaching for a packet of cereal can stimulate thoughts like 'What are you doing? You don't need that now, he or she isn't here any more, he doesn't need the cereal'. Meanwhile, the person's heart may respond with 'Don't listen, put the cereal in the trolley'. They may feel on some level that if they put the cereal in the trolley, there is some sense of that person being alive. If they leave the cereal on the shelf, that seems like confirming their death.

Confusion, distress and tears may make the bereaved person abandon the trolley, running from the supermarket in despair. No wonder that panic attacks in such situations are common. It is helpful to shop with a caring person who can provide reassurance that these feelings will eventually pass, that, despite their discomfort, they are a normal part of the process of grief.

In the beginning, pain seems to be a constant, overwhelming companion until we gradually become familiar with its intensity, and therefore less fearful. The time spent in peaks of pain slowly decreases and the time between peaks becomes longer, providing necessary periods of relief. Initially, relief may be short lived, perhaps just minutes of respite which gradually stretch into hours, days, weeks. We don't 'get over' grief — it just changes shape and intensity as we learn how to live in the physical absence of the person or persons we love.

Anniversaries and special dates

During the first year, and sometimes for many years, the approach of special dates may cause intense pain. Birthdays, anniversaries and familiar celebrations and rituals which may have been happy occasions may now be the antithesis of the joy they once were. It may be helpful to do something different on those special days, perhaps arrange to be in the company of caring people, especially if they are able to understand if it becomes necessary to change plans at the last minute.

Many people still want to buy cards, bake cakes, or choose gifts for the person who died, all of which is normal and healthy and not a denial of death as some concerned others might imply. Do whatever feels right.

One year later: the anniversary of the death

The anniversary reaction may begin around eleven months after the death, often indicated by a return to the intense feelings and confused thoughts which are common in the early days. Bodily distress is common. For example, headaches, nausea, backache, chest pain (particularly if the deceased died from a heart attack), vomiting, diarrhoea, extreme tiredness, and period problems in pre-menopausal women. Grief affects every part of us — body, mind and spirit. The feeling that every cell is hurting can return in great intensity around the anniversary date, and many people are vulnerable at that time to infection because of the impact of grief on our immune systems. It is common for the bereaved to experience symptoms of the condition which caused the person's death, even if that was an accident.

It is useful to prepare for the anniversary time, particularly in subsequent years, by avoiding over-tiredness, perhaps taking vitamin supplements, or having a massage.

Make plans to spend time with caring people in

situations in which you feel comfortable, where you can just be yourself. Don't rely too heavily on the memories of others, because they may let you down, albeit unintentionally. Remind important people of the date, ask for help if you are able, and accept help that is offered.

Support at this time may make it easier to confront pain by sharing it, and later to decrease its intensity. However, if avoidance helps you to survive, then that may be the right path for you. Just do whatever works, as long as it isn't harmful to you or to others.

Build in contingency plans. For example, if you think you would prefer to be alone on the anniversary day, try to keep someone 'on notice' in case you change your mind at the last minute.

Grief and the body

Physical reactions

In conjunction with emotional responses to grief there are a host of physical responses, all of them designed to reduce pain to a manageable degree. When someone we love dies, our body produces a number of narcotic-like chemicals similar to heroin or morphine. These pain-killing chemicals help to produce the numbing experience most of us feel at the beginning. For those who cry, these chemicals are released in tears, which is why it is important for others not to try to prevent crying. For others, soothing chemicals will be released through physical exercise.

Gradually, as the weeks go by, the production of these chemicals decreases and around four to six weeks later they are significantly lower. The resulting increase in distress at this time is the result of greater awareness of the reality of death, coupled with the body's attempt (through increased crying) to produce more chemicals to aid survival.

It works. How often do you sit down, have a good cry, and feel better afterwards?

It is important for support people to understand the benefit of crying, and not only allow it, but on occasions facilitate tears by asking the right kinds of question — those that most others avoid for fear of upsetting bereaved people. Crying is not 'going downhill'. Rather, it is the reverse — attempting the long haul with whatever internal and external help is available to assist the process. At this time it is important to be kind to ourselves — to let go, as much as we are able, of our need to be in control.

Not eating, not sleeping

Not eating and not sleeping are also healthy aspects of grief.

The body chemicals previously mentioned can also have a relaxing effect on some muscles, for example, those used for digestion. Because these muscles are slowed down, the body says to itself 'don't eat because you can't get rid of the waste'. Our bodies do not need the same amount of food they would need in normal circumstances, and loss of appetite allows our energy to be redirected to the muscles involved in fight of flight. However, it is important that the food we eat is nutritious and easily digested. Fresh fruit and vegetables in small quantities are particularly helpful, as are foods like yoghurt and other soft comfort foods.

There are many reasons for not sleeping, one being the amount of adrenalin produced by grief and remaining trapped in our bodies. Adrenalin is the stress chemical produced when we sense danger — to prepare us for fight or flight. Bereavement and trauma can be regarded as the most potent form of stress the body has to withstand, so we produce enormous amounts of adrenalin to help us 'cope'. Our muscles, loaded with adrenalin, become tense and tight. Our heart (myocardium, or heart muscle) becomes tense and beats more rapidly, producing palpitations, making us ready for action. Nothing happens of course and we are left primed, just in case, which makes sleep difficult.

In previous generations and in some other cultures we might have used a significant amount of adrenalin in the grieving process. For example, we might, as a family or cultural group, have sat down around the body and wept and wailed for three days and three nights, at the end of which time we probably wouldn't have had a wail left in our bodies. We wouldn't have needed tranquillisers or sleeping tablets, but would have just collapsed from exhaustion.

Instead of taking drugs or using alcohol, we would probably all be better off using adrenalin to go for a long walk, preferably with a friend who will allow us to talk about whatever is on our minds at the time. Gardening, housework, bathing the dog, mowing the lawn, washing the car are all activities that can help. However, these are usually the things that family, friends and neighbours tend to do as their way of saying 'I care'. It would probably be more helpful if they did these things with us, instead of for us.

Many people find massage helpful when they are feeling distressed. Massage, one of the oldest and gentlest forms of therapy, when provided by an ethical, trained practitioner, relaxes tight muscles, often facilitates crying, and allows us to feel nurtured. Find a masseur who can resist the temptation to 'counsel' at the same time, or try to 'fix things' if your feelings are close to the surface. Perhaps you or a friend could explain to them that you may need to cry, and for them not to feel alarmed or need to do anything about your tears. It is important to be allowed to 'just be'.

Bodily distress

As already mentioned, any bodily system or organ can be affected by grief to a large extent or lesser degree. Effects may range from skin eruptions, gastro-intestinal disturbances like heartburn, dyspepsia, constipation and diarrhoea, through to severe, incapacitating symptoms such as chest pain, muscle spasms and migraine. We have already noted that many symptoms experienced by bereaved people may mimic symptoms of the person who died, or be manifestations of what we imagine they might have experienced.

In a situation we are familiar with, both mother and daughter experienced severe chest pain after their father and grandfather died from a heart attack. Another example of chest pains in response to sudden death is a woman who was referred for counselling six months after her teenage son died in a motor vehicle accident. Doctors couldn't find any physical cause for her recurrent pain. In conversation, Mrs X said her son had been driving his recently acquired second-hand car when it apparently went out of control on a bend, going over an embankment and finally crashing into a tree. When asked to tell how her son actually died, she gave a graphic description of how he was impaled on the steering wheel. As she described the manner of his death, she struck herself on the chest, immediately producing the now familiar pain. As she wept, she made her own connection between the pain and her son's death.

Another example of this common and frightening experience concerns a death from cancer. A mother of two young children, a girl aged ten and a boy aged eight, died after a protracted illness lasting a number of years. The final symptom of her worsening condition was cancer-related obstruction of her bowel, discovered after she was admitted to hospital for investigation of constipation. No curative treatment could be offered and she died a short time later. Ten days after the death, her ten-year-old woke in the night with intense abdominal pain. She was taken to hospital, where it was discovered that she had acute, severe constipation with the same symptoms that her mother had experienced before her death. The girl's constipation was treated and there were no long-term difficulties.

Whenever unusual physical symptoms appear after bereavement it is always important to have them checked medically before seeking counselling or following other management plans.

Emotional reactions

Anger versus aggression

Anger, like all other responses, is a survival mechanism. It may be intense and frightening to self or others, and may result from the nature of the death, its suddenness, or perceived preventability. It may also result from some behaviour of the deceased prior to death — for example, risk-taking, drug use, drunkenness, rebellion or carelessness.

There may have been medical mismanagement, or we might imagine that is the case and project our feelings of guilt or regret onto another. Anger may be felt by both men and women, but is more likely to be expressed by men, and is usually most obvious around the time of notification of the death or when numbness begins to subside, even if momentarily. Unfortunately anger is sometimes directed towards those who are closest — family and friends, or a previously trusted medical team.

If, as a carer, we are alarmed by a bereaved person's anger, it is important to ask ourselves, 'If I took this person's anger away, what would be left?' If the answer is 'Nothing', it is important not to stop its safe expression. Anger expressed openly in a safe and accepting environment will gradually decrease in intensity, even though similar words may continue to be used. Physical activities like sport, gardening, running or housework can be helpful in using anger energy. Alternatively, a punching bag can be helpful for some people, or letting fly in the garage or other safe place with old crockery.

Unexpressed anger can build up on the inside and explode at inappropriate times, or cause later problems like the physical symptoms already described.

Sometimes anger can be directed at the informant of the death — the proverbial 'bearer of bad tidings'. It is usually helpful (when possible) to safeguard close relationships by having an outsider be the informant of bad news — whether diagnosis or death. In our society, we tend to believe that it is better for a husband to tell his wife of a child's death, or parents to tell their children of the death of someone they love. We may then wonder why the informant is pushed away, not understanding that it is a defence mechanism, a vain attempt to push away the impact of painful news. Giving the news symbolically kills the person who was alive until that moment, so the informant can be unconsciously perceived as the perpetrator.

If a bereaved person is aggressive and inflicting physical or psychological harm to another, then social restraints need to be applied. Bereavement does not make people aggressive — aggression is a pre-existing personality trait and no caring person should have to be on the receiving end, no matter how much the grieving person is hurting.

It is important not to confuse raised voices, screaming or appropriate hitting of inanimate objects with aggression. The intensity of anger experienced may be frightening and unfamiliar to the bereaved person and to those supporting them, but it is just another way of expressing pain.

Guilt

Bereaved people often say that they feel guilty. They need someone to listen to their guilt, without trying to make them feel better, without trying to take their guilt away. Words like 'Come on, you mustn't blame yourself', 'It wasn't your fault' or 'He/she wouldn't want you to blame yourself' are usually more irritating than helpful.

As bereaved people, we often wish we could turn back the clock, do something differently, do more, say less, prevent the death from occurring, no matter how unrealistic that wish may be. Imagining doing things differently allows us another opportunity to express our love, another way of saying 'there isn't anything I wouldn't have done to keep this person alive'. At these times, most of us need a caring person simply to listen when we say that we wish we had just one more time to say 'I love you', or say we are sorry for taking our eyes off the child near the pool, or for falling asleep while driving the car. The person experiencing guilt needs to be able to tell their story, tell it the way they wish it had been, apologise, repent, confess — to be able to say 'sorry' from the heart.

Bereaved people don't express guilt in order to make others feel uncomfortable or helpless — they just do what their bodies and hearts need them to do. When that happens, the intensity of their guilt feelings will usually decrease over time, while they may still continue to use the same words. For example, guilt language will usually change from 'I feel so guilty for...' to 'Whenever I think about X I still feel guilty'.

This subtle change is reassuring in that it indicates that guilt is only being felt when the thought is there — not every waking moment.

Depression

Depression is a clinical term used to indicate a psychiatric condition for which there is known treatment, usually of a chemical nature. Grief may appear to the unskilled observer to be the same as depression, but there are many differences. Put simply, depression is 'of the head' — that is, an illness involving the way we think — and grief is 'of the heart', the way we feel.

Passionate sadness is a more appropriate way of describing grief, and passionate sadness does not require chemical treatment. Passionate sadness requires a compassionate listener, a safe environment, opportunities to repeat stories over and over from slightly different angles, and gradual development of management strategies that come from understanding who the bereaved person is and all they have been, rather than an externally applied prescription.

Grief tends to stimulate behaviour that makes it easy for the untrained or inexperienced carer to confuse it with depression. For example, loss of appetite, difficulty sleeping, lack of energy and motivation, bouts of weeping and sadness, lack of meaning in life, and occasional expressions of 'I wish I was dead' look and sound like depression, and can scare caring others to push the bereaved person to prematurely seek medical help — to 'take something'. Before going down that path it is wise to see a skilled bereavement counsellor who should be able to carry out a 'grief assessment' and explain the difference between depression and passionate sadness.

Despair

Despair tends to occur when numbness wears off, when the reality and foreverness of death begins to penetrate, and the bereaved person loses all hope of seeing that loved person again. Even when bereaved people have strong religious beliefs that include being reunited in an afterlife, most people long to feel, hold, hear, their loved person again *now*. Despair may last for a long time for some, come and go at intervals for others, but it won't remain as a constant feeling forever. Recovery from unbearable yearning may be slow, but with the right support, acceptance, understanding, and gradual ability to re-access our own internal resources, most of us will eventually re-experience hope.

Replacement

People often experience grief as a void, a disfiguration — 'like part of me has gone'. It is easy to believe that all will be well if the void can be filled, for example by marrying again if a partner has died, or having another baby if the loss is a result of miscarriage, stillbirth, neonatal death, or death of a young child. There are usually plenty of caring others to offer advice along these lines, often using the words 'you're young enough to…'.

It is usually in bereaved people's best interests to ignore such advice, well meaning as it might be, and, where possible, avoid making major decisions in the first thirteen to eighteen months. Major decisions include selling the family home, remarrying, becoming pregnant again, changing jobs or ending friendships. In the early days, weeks, months, nothing can really fill the emotional void, although it does help if a number of others (not one person alone) provide some of the important things that the deceased person contributed to the bereaved person's life and wellbeing. These needs are individually determined and depend on the nature of the previous relationship, but may include love, friendship, physical touch (when non-exploitative), money, support, a listening ear, understanding and acceptance, as well as practical help.

Not all help is in the best interests of the bereaved person. For example, well-intentioned friends and family members may decide to be helpful by preparing an abundance of food and almost 'force feeding' the bereaved person. They may decide to pack up and dispose of the deceased person's belongings without consultation, on occasions while the bereaved person is at the funeral. We know of situations where family members have packed up a nursery while the mother of a stillborn baby is still in hospital, believing that the sight of baby clothes and furniture would only cause pain. In doing this, they deprived the mother of the opportunity to go through the belongings in her own time, reliving memories, hopes and dreams, shedding warm, painful, therapeutic tears in the process. Imagine a mother packing up the nursery, holding baby clothes against her face, remembering the feel of her baby kicking inside her — bringing her unborn child to life for just a moment. Imagine a wife packing up her husband's clothes, finding a theatre ticket in his jacket pocket, then sitting down, reminiscing about that and other outings, briefly bringing him and their relationship back to life, then crying painful tears as she reminds herself that she will never get to share those outings again.

In these and other painful scenarios, the bereaved person may have to abandon the task when enough is enough, only to return again and again when ready, perhaps unconsciously needing to stimulate healing tears again. Clothes may be kept for a long time, some given away and others kept, or never given away — there is no absolute right or wrong, only what is right for each person.

Bereaved people often talk about belongings they choose to keep as memories of the deceased. These may range from letters, cards, hats, jumpers, handkerchiefs, pipes, perfume, aftershave, pyjamas and jewellery to the last thing used by that person. Observers may become concerned about what is kept, but are usually less so if the object is of monetary value. For example, if you keep Grandpa's gold watch and chain and wear it around your neck as a piece of jewellery, that's OK, but if you decide to keep his old gardening jumper because it smells like him and reminds you of happy times spent together in the garden, they are likely to think that is abnormal or 'creepy'.

Many bereaved people feel as if they spend most of their time trying to make other people feel comfortable. They quickly learn how to wear a stoic, public face and save more obvious grief for private moments. Other people's needs and discomfort aside, it can be helpful to wear a 'public face' to protect ourselves from thoughtless comments when we are particularly vulnerable, but it is equally important not to change behaviour that is especially meaningful to us to suit the needs of others. Do what feels right, but don't always tell other people what you choose to do.

Back to the beginning

The immediate needs of the bereaved

You may have just been informed that someone you love has died. Shock and disbelief are usually initial reactions. It is difficult to acknowledge this information, let alone fully understand or believe what you are hearing. You may feel faint, weak and overwhelmed; the words 'dead, dead, dead' playing over and over in your mind.

Every part of you may want to respond with 'No! No! No!' Everything seems surreal.

Seeing the body — yes or no?

In the midst of this unfamiliar and confusing reaction, someone, perhaps a nurse, doctor or relative, may say, 'Would you like to see his/her body?' On the inside you may say, 'No, I don't want to see him/her dead, he/ she can't be dead.' On the outside your response might simply be 'No', meaning 'I don't want to see him dead, I'd rather see him alive'. If you have said 'No', and others have taken your reaction at face value, you may have deprived yourself of important time to spend with the person you love. It is understandably a very difficult decision for most people to have to make at this time.

If we don't get to be with the person who has died, we may find it harder to integrate the truth of their death, leaving us in partial denial, perhaps permanently. This denial may or may not cause problems, the outcome often dependent on the degree of intimacy in the relationship.

An example of partial denial can be found in the death of Harold Holt, former Prime Minister of Australia, who disappeared while swimming, believed drowned. His body was never recovered. At the time of his disappearance, and to this day, rumours abound asserting that he was not really dead, but had been picked up by a mini-submarine from Russia or the CIA, that he was a spy for China and had returned there, and many other variations on the theme. We have no way of proving or disproving the rumours because we have no body to 'view', leaving most of us in partial denial.

This is not a problem for people who didn't know him or have an intimate personal relationship with him, but for his family and close friends, this denial could be incapacitating and affect the quality of their lives. They may have been left with endless questions, such as 'What if he isn't dead?' 'Maybe he will just walk in the door one day?' They may have said things like 'Not knowing is even worse than seeing him dead'.

Many people over the years have told us that not being 100% sure, as a result of not seeing ('seeing is believing') the body of the person they love, has been the most painful aspect of their loss. There are, of course, people who don't need to see or spend time with the body of the person they love in order to believe they are dead, or to learn how to live with their grief. However, it is hard to know in advance who will be OK and who will be adversely affected by not spending time with their loved one after death. For this reason it is best when we are in a supportive role to err on the side of gently encouraging bereaved people by saying a version of 'I think it will be beneficial in the long term for you to spend time with your husband/wife/mother/child before you go'.

Caring supporters can confidentially make such a

statement, if not from their own personal or professional experience, then from the experience of specialists working in the field of death, dying and bereavement. As painfully sad as it might be for the bereaved person, it does present an opportunity to acknowledge reality, for senses to adjust to change, even though most of us at this time don't want to acknowledge or accept what has occurred. Most people are later glad they have had this important opportunity, even those who have been initially reluctant.

Before 'viewing the body'

There are several important steps that can help to make what funeral directors call 'viewing the body' (spending time with a loved person who has died) a more beneficial experience. First, it helps if someone less emotionally affected by the death has had their own experience first, and is later able to provide a description of the scene family members are about to enter. Attention to detail is especially important if we are taking children into this situation, but it can be helpful for all of us to have someone explain what we will see on entering the room, and what our senses might register, for example — temperature and smell.

The following case history (people Mal counselled) is an example.

Marie, aged forty and divorced, had three children — a boy Brian aged nine, and two girls — Samantha aged seven and Cathy aged five. Marie died following a two-year history of cancer. Mal was involved with the family prior to Marie's death, and was asked to remain involved afterwards to help support the children. The children were encouraged to go with him to spend time with their mother, who they knew was dead.

When they arrived at the funeral director's, the conversation went something like this:

MAL: *'You know we're here because Mummy died?'*
CHILDREN: *'Yes.'*
MAL: *'Have you ever seen anyone who has died?'*
CHILDREN: *'No.'*
MAL: *'Well, when we go in to see Mummy, she'll probably look a little bit different to the last time you saw her.'*
CHILDREN: *'What do you mean, different?'*
MAL: *'Well, when you are alive and if you are white-skinned like me, your blood helps to make you the colour you are. If I grip my thumb around the middle and squeeze it, you can see that it goes a pink colour. That's because I'm squeezing the blood up to the surface. But if I extend my hand as much as I can and straighten out my palm, you can*

see that my palm goes a much lighter colour in the middle. That's because I'm squeezing the blood out, it's not moving around much any more. When we die it's a bit like that, because the blood doesn't move around our body any more and we look really pale. Also, when we're alive, our blood helps keep us warm, but when we're dead, we can't feel the cold, so we don't need to be warm any more. If you touch Mummy when we go in, she'll feel cold to you, but she can't feel it because she is dead.'

In such circumstances it is important to use language that is suitable to the individual person, but the way of explaining, the content of the message, is similar irrespective of the age of the bereaved person. Because the scenario above was in a funeral director's, Mal went on to say, 'When we go inside, Mummy will be in a coffin, with the lid off. Have any of you seen a coffin before?'

He then described the room, the coffin and its position, how their mother was lying, and what she was wearing.

It is important to explain the situation in detail so that the person who is going to 'view' the body is not unduly shocked by the dead person's appearance — that they have time to protect their 'core' by rehearsing images in their mind.

As already explained, one reason for encouraging someone to 'view the body' is to enhance reality, but another is to allow the bereaved to say and do whatever is important to them, so they are not left unnecessarily with unfinished business. As a support person, you could encourage them by saying something like 'If there's anything you wish to say, or anything you wish you'd had a chance to say before he/she died, now is the time'.

People often want to say things like 'I love you' or 'I'm so sorry'. Others may want to express angry thoughts and feelings that have been bottled up, perhaps for ages. For example, 'I told you not to do it you silly old so and so'. All are about love and sorrow, expressed differently.

A support person could then encourage further expression by asking, 'If he/she could hear what you just said, how would they respond?'

This important experience should take place where it is safe for bereaved people to express grief openly, without censure, and should never be hurried. Afterwards, the bereaved person or persons should be encouraged to sit down for a while to talk about their reactions to the experience, or just to sit quietly if talking is difficult.

What the bereaved person needs

One of the greatest needs of all bereaved people is to have access to someone who will take a risk and be involved — someone who is not afraid of intense feelings, but who will encourage their expression, confident that this is part of the 'healing' process. We use the word 'healing' not to imply that grief is an illness that can be cured, but in acknowledgement that in the early days, weeks, months, years, every part of one's being can feel raw, inflamed and vulnerable.

People in support roles should resist any temptation to say 'I know how you feel', even if they have also experienced the pain of grief. We can never really know how another feels — we can only use our own experience to help us sensitively imagine a little of another person's distress. It is much more helpful to ask a bereaved person to 'tell me what is happening for you'.

Permission to grieve

Bereaved people are very vulnerable and susceptible to the criticisms and judgements of others. Comments are often given unasked about how the bereaved person should grieve, demonstrating in that process how little those other people really understand about its nature.

Grief is dynamic and ever-changing — in shape and intensity — determined by everything the bereaved was before this event, the nature of their relationship with the deceased, their physical and emotional health, age, and the environment in which they live.

At this time we all need to be allowed to be ourselves, to do what feels right for us, not spend scarce energy trying to conform to the needs and expectations of others.

Many of us need to be allowed to cry, others have never been 'cryers' and are probably not about to become 'cryers' now. There still appears to be a pervasive myth in our society that crying is bad and must be stopped or prevented. On the contrary, if we are the kind of people who cry readily, it is in our best interests to be allowed or encouraged to cry when grief needs expression in this way. We have mentioned several times already that it can be detrimental to most people in the long run to be forced to bottle up tears that have the potential to calm and soothe.

Retaining individuality

The bereaved person is the only one who can feel what they feel, think what they think, and know the best way of expressing whatever they are experiencing.

Others affected by the death will have their own way of grieving, of expressing feelings which may be different. There is no right or wrong — grief just 'is'.

Some people feel like taking to their bed for a couple of days; some want to stay with a friend for a short time; others feel like cursing, yelling, screaming, crying or withdrawing — all understandable needs and grief responses. If friends give unwanted advice, listen if necessary, but continue to do what feels right for you — if it works, don't fix it.

Friends are usually trying to help, but that doesn't mean you have to behave according to their prescription. When possible, let friends and family know that it is OK to talk about the person who has died, OK to mention their name. People often don't know what to do or say, and giving them permission to talk about, ask questions, say the name of the dead person can decrease tension and make it less likely for awkwardness to produce clichés or unwanted advice.

'Coping'

The word 'coping' is often a misleading judgement, used inappropriately in relation to grief. Observers who make comments about a grieving person along the lines of 'He/she seems to be coping really well', or 'He/she isn't coping very well' tend to base their ability to judge *your* wellbeing on how *they* feel about what you are doing. For example, if you are very obviously distressed and crying, you are likely to be described as 'not coping very well'. If you don't express your grief overtly or don't show more grief than the observer is comfortable with, they are likely to describe you as 'coping very well'. It is also possible to show too little grief for their comfort level. If you don't cry or appear filled with sorrow or pain, they don't have a role and may consequently describe you as cold.

The title of this book — *Coping with Grief* — is an attempt to redefine what coping really means. When any of us are newly bereaved, we are 'coping' if we can keep breathing, put one foot after the other, get out of bed, dress ourselves, and attend to essential tasks even if on automatic pilot. We all just do our best to survive what initially feels unsurvivable, and often need to reassure ourselves that we do know what is best for us, that we are *not* going mad.

The funeral

For many of you, the funeral will be long past before you get to read this book. However, the information provided below can still serve several purposes. First, it can allow an opportunity to review how the funeral was for you, whether it met your needs at the time, or if in hindsight there are things you wish had been different. If regrets cause you distress, it can help to talk these over with a friend or family member you trust, or perhaps a bereavement counsellor. If you are able to describe how you would like it to have been, your body will respond as if that version had indeed happened, and produce the chemicals necessary to help you feel more at peace.

Second, you may find ways of answering children's questions, or of justifying some of your choices to others if they make annoying comments or ask probing questions. And finally, it may enable you in the future to be supportive of friends and relatives when they are in the situation you are now experiencing.

The function of the funeral (a service held with the body of the deceased present) is threefold: first, to pay tribute to the deceased person in a way that appropriately reflects the life they have lived; second, to reinforce the reality of the death for those who are grieving; and third, to bring together relatives and friends to share an experience which has the capacity to re-establish group relationships. These relationships are an important part of the process of learning how to live with the physical absence of the person who has died.

Human beings do not live in a vacuum. Our speech, values and behaviour — the very meaning of our lives — are derived from our association with one another. The death of one individual affects the lives of all others in that social grouping and the funeral ritual is designed to meet their needs at a time of shared distress.

Because this rite of passage is an important aspect of the healing process, involvement should be available to all who mourn, especially those most affected by the death — spouse, children, parents, siblings and close friends. If, for any reason, one of the significant mourners is unable to attend because delaying the funeral is not possible, it is helpful to record the service on DVD or audio tape. When possible, photos should be taken, and flowers and cards kept so that the person who was absent can eventually feel included in the process. Some people find it helpful to hold a later memorial service (one held in the absence of the body of the deceased) so that everyone has the opportunity to express their grief publicly and feel included in all important aspects of the process.

Children too should be included, no matter what their age at the time, and encouraged where possible to be actively involved. Their grief behaviour may be different to that of adults but their internal process is much the same, feeling all the same emotions that adults experience, and just as intensely. Being allowed to write or draw messages to the deceased, perhaps placing them in the coffin, reading at the funeral if they are able and willing, can give them an opportunity to express in behaviour what may not be possible for them in words. We often try to protect children by keeping them away from funerals for fear they may become upset, forgetting that being upset is appropriate when someone they love dies. Preventing them from being part of all important aspects of dying and death can leave them with resentment that carries on into adult life.

If we look honestly at our own motives for shielding children from being part of these rites of passage, we may find that it is sometimes to protect ourselves, not them. We may fear and try to avoid the simplicity and directness of their responses, their probing or unanswerable questions, and in so doing, prevent them from learning, in the safety of their own kinship circle, about death as part of life.

From a practical perspective, funeral services can be conducted almost anywhere, by almost anyone. We may choose a church, chapel, funeral director's, crematorium, park, garden or private home. It is important to remember that if you wish to hold the funeral service in a public place such as a park or beach you will need council permission. It is customary, though not essential, to engage the services of a funeral director who can attend to details, leaving the family free to grieve without inhibition or distraction.

Because a funeral is not a legal ceremony like a wedding, it is possible to use a friend, relative or celebrant to lead the ceremony, but whoever you choose, it is important that they conduct the service in the way you wish.

As mentioned earlier, many people feel pressured by themselves or others into having the funeral as soon as possible in the mistaken belief that once 'it' is over, mourners will be able to put 'it' all behind them and get on with life.

Slowing down and taking time to plan a meaningful service is usually of much more benefit in the long term. It allows time to develop a greater understanding of the reality of the death, and increases the likelihood that the bereaved will remember important details later. It is valuable to most people to choose music and readings that are a multi-dimensional reflection of the life of the deceased, select appropriate flowers, and choose photos to display. Time usually allows most of us to be more assertive about arranging to have a church, chapel or crematorium available for longer than the specified time, even if it means paying a bit extra for the privilege. A service cut short does not necessarily decrease distress.

Many people choose to hold an informal gathering after the service — a wake, or funeral party as children tend to call it. If you are able to make yourself receptive to the love and compassion offered by family and friends at this time, you may find surprising comfort in the telling of stories, sharing experiences, and laughing as everyone remembers fun aspects of the deceased person's life. It is important to many to acknowledge openly how they have been touched by that individual, what they will remember always, and perhaps crying again as a group when awareness of that person's physical absence resurfaces. The shared intimacy of these gatherings often leave bereaved people feeling 'high' for a little while — a feeling that helps later survival.

It is normal and healthy to feel the kind of 'high' we are describing, and certainly nothing to feel guilty about. We learn in this way that happiness and sadness can co-exist — one doesn't cancel out the other.

And finally, contrary to hopes and dreams, and perhaps romantic versions of death portrayed in books or movies, death doesn't tend to resolve family conflict. In fact, dying, death, funerals and grief have the capacity to exaggerate whatever pre-existed, meaning that conflict may become more pronounced, estrangement even more painful, outspoken and sharp-tongued folk even more so. Many of us may experience family dynamics that leave us with thoughts and feelings that have the capacity to complicate our grief. In this instance, the help of a competent bereavement counsellor can be invaluable.

The context

Preparatory grief

When we know in advance that someone we love has a terminal illness, our grief usually begins from the time we hear the bad news. We are likely to react initially with shock and a desire to push the news away with the now familiar words, 'No, it can't be true. Maybe someone will find a cure. Maybe we can get a second opinion, find an alternative treatment. Maybe a miracle will happen'.

If the person who is ill is open and honest, and makes conversation about their diagnosis and prognosis possible once the shock subsides, we may be able to speak with little reservation about the impending threat. We may be able to share love, fears, pain and comfort in a way that prevents a build-up of emotion, allowing us to prepare for the inevitable in practical as well as emotional ways.

Preparatory grief may allow us to say and do all the things that are important to us and our relationship with the dying person, to reduce the possibility of any unfinished business that has the potential to later complicate grief. Some couples or families cope best by not saying out loud what they all know is happening, because that is the way they have dealt with distress in the past. Whatever our personal style, we may find ourselves beginning to distance a little, usually unconsciously, as we prepare to take over roles the dying person may have fulfilled, and tasks they may have carried out. In this sense, we will probably have less distance to travel in practical terms after the death occurs, but it doesn't mean that we will have used up our 'grief quota', and be ready to move on with life.

Death is almost always experienced as sudden, no matter how much warning we have, and despite some initial relief that the dying person is now free of pain, grief is still grief, and usually no less raw because of foreknowledge. Occasionally, preparatory grief can become complicated. For example, a respected medical practitioner may have estimated survival time as three months, or up to a year, yet the dying person may still be alive two years later. If we imagine this scenario in a couple relationship where one of the partners has a terminal diagnosis, we could imagine both partners unconsciously beginning to distance, losing some of the intimacy that has been an important part of their previous relationship. The well partner begins to pace themselves, doing everything possible in the predicted timeframe, only to find themselves worn out and empty of resources into the second year. They may find themselves becoming irritable, almost resentful of the prolonged dying process, and later feel overwhelmed with guilt and regret. Most people want to retain closeness for as long as possible, to soak up all the memories they want to be able to draw on in the future, but may fear reinvesting in the relationship. Professional support can be very helpful in these situations to enable the relationship to be sustained for as long as possible.

Sometimes distance is created in the dying process because of personality change, for example with some brain tumours. When this happens, the original relationship is lost long before the death occurs, stimulating grief on an almost daily basis as each physical function or personality trait is lost. Often there is no opportunity to stay still long enough to process daily changes and grieve for each loss as it occurs. It may not be until some time after the death that the surviving person has the time or energy to process all they have experienced.

Children also experience preparatory grief, even when they haven't been told the truth about diagnosis and prognosis. They may begin to distance to protect themselves, and in doing so can attract criticism for being cold and unfeeling. Dying children may also sense more about their illness than adults realise. They may pretend they don't know, or try to act positively to protect adults they care about, even their doctors. Whether the diagnosis and prognosis is about them or someone they love, it is best to ensure that they have access to truthful information. Someone will tell them, or they will overhear adult conversation, or simply react to and interpret tension in the environment. If information is learned via others, particularly if it is given unkindly by another, they tend to lose trust in important adults in their lives.

It is understandable that parents and other caring adults want to protect children from the seriousness of their own or another's illness, but protection is not helpful in the long term. Fortunately these days, many paediatric staff are well aware of the ability of children to comprehend the seriousness of their own illness, as are oncologists who may be treating their parent or sibling, meaning that children's needs for truth and inclusion are more likely to be respected.

Children and grief

Children, like adults, learn best how to understand and live with death in the absence of family sorrow. For example, parents should ideally teach their children about death as they teach them language and facts about the natural world of which we are all part. They can be shown dead or dying plants, insects, birds and animals, and allowed to feel them as they observe that death can mean changing colour, not being able to move, breathe, eat, feel, make sound or respond to touch. We can help them to become familiar with the word 'dead', not euphemisms, and to develop a sense of reverence for all life and respect for what has died.

We can gradually teach children that we are all connected to each other, that whatever affects one person in our family or social group affects all other members. When one of those significant people dies, those of us still alive may continue to honour them by remembering the important things they contributed to life and the family, the lessons we have learned from them and how we might express some of their ideals in our own lives. We can show them that people die but our relationships with them live forever.

We can show children that death presents an opportunity for family and friends to draw closer together in love and affection, providing comfort, hope and support in times of crisis. If we include them in family grieving as fully as possible, we can make an important contribution to their social development, even if they don't understand everything that is happening. Children can also be a source of strength and comfort for adults at this time, with their simple, direct approach, and their ability to refocus adult attention onto their needs in the here and now.

If children are sent away to stay with friends or relatives at this time, they will return to an altered family, a family that has a shared experience of grief. The child may feel excluded, their grief unchanged from when they were last with their family, and they may feel resentful without understanding why.

Young children are used to hearing and fantasising about death from reading fairy tales and watching TV shows. They are often more able to talk about death than adults, perhaps because they have a different awareness of the world around them, and in their early years, little understanding of the foreverness of death.

Euphemisms like 'We've lost Daddy' or 'Grandad is asleep now', or 'Nana passed away' will be interpreted literally and cause distress and confusion rather than give comfort. Any reference to death being 'sleep' can make young children afraid of closing their eyes, and anxious at bed time.

Mal remembers going to a funeral director's with a family after their friend's child died. As they were leaving the chapel, one of the adults said, 'Didn't he look peaceful, just like he was asleep.' Their eight-year-old son, who was beside Mal, whispered, 'He didn't look like he was asleep to me. He looked dead.' He went on to explain that when the dead child went to bed he always slept bunched up, and he wasn't like that in his coffin.

Children need to be told facts in simple straightforward language, appropriate for their age. They need to know that questions are not taboo, that they will be given answers or that answers will be found for them if adults don't know the answer. Before answering a child's questions, it is always important for adults to ask first, 'What do you understand about Mummy's/Daddy's/Nana's/Billie's illness?' Their response not only allows adults thinking time, and an opportunity to correct misinformation, but ensures that it is the right question we are responding to.

In their early years, children do best with simple, factual explanations about what death is, and what happens after death. Complex, adult ideas and religious beliefs require competence in abstract thinking, and are best kept for when the child is older. For example, they will interpret heaven as a literal place, filled with toys and other goodies, much more desirable than living on earth. It should not be surprising then when children use language that can sound as if they have suicidal thoughts, expressing a desire to join whoever has died in this magical place. We need to help them sustain belief in the positive aspects of life as we know it, and remain confident that we will have plenty of time to teach them whatever belief system is important to us as they mature. Our values are usually best communicated via our behaviour — behaviour has more power than any words we may use.

It is sometimes tempting to tell children that 'Mummy is a star in heaven'. That is not a truth and can later contribute to a child learning distrust in adult words. It is better to say something like 'When we look at the stars we can think about Mummy because she was/is a star in our lives'. There are many ways to remember and honour the person who has died, to keep them feeling close, and to keep the relationship alive in the child's mind and heart, but they need to be truthful.

Children learn about grief and how to express feelings by observing the behaviour of adults. It is important not to hide our tears, but children may need reassurance after witnessing intense weeping or anger; to hear that 'Nothing bad is going to happen because I am crying/shouting — I'm just sad that X has died, and I miss them'.

Children usually express their feelings differently to adults, crying into their pillow at night, embarrassed by others seeing their tears, especially their peers. They may cry disproportionately in response to some minor event, like kicking their toe or someone teasing them, and many other instances that give them an excuse to release feelings they may have bottled up. Their grief is more likely to be expressed in behaviour, like acting out — often an attempt to draw grieving adults back into familiar caretaking — or perhaps in role playing. Young children may play death-related games around funerals, burials and so on in an attempt to become familiar with and integrate their understanding of death. Their emotional state may change quickly — sad and withdrawn one moment — playing happily with friends in another.

Children, like adults, usually need to spend time with friends, perhaps talking to them about the person who died, and going over the details about how they died, sometimes acting these details out in ways that seem disturbing to adults. However odd their behaviour may seem, it is a normal healthy response which takes care of an internal process. However, if grieving children become aggressive or rebellious, adults (parents, teachers, grandparents) need to make sure that firm boundaries remain in place. Whatever behaviour was unacceptable before the death (or diagnosis) occurred remains unacceptable afterwards. Boundaries help children to feel safe, secure in the knowledge that some things remain unchanged, that someone is in control of some things in life. Grief is an explanation, not an excuse for disrespectful behaviour in children or adults.

Sometimes, children and young people may appear not to be grieving at all. They may laugh and play with friends as if nothing has changed, older children spending time on their mobile phones sending text messages, or arranging the usual outings. This is simply their way of dealing with death anxiety, of reassuring themselves that they can survive, that life will go on, despite grief. It doesn't mean that they didn't love the person who died, or that they don't miss them — it certainly doesn't mean that they aren't feeling.

Many children feel guilty when people they love become seriously ill or die, especially if they are very young and still in the developmental period of magic thinking. They may think 'If only I had been a good boy, Daddy mightn't have died', and many similar thoughts, believing that their behaviour or thoughts have the power to kill. If your child or children in your care make these statements, or you suspect they might be thinking along these lines, don't rush in with reassurance but listen first to their fears, then give them facts that may help decrease the intensity of their guilt. As painful as it is to see your child hurting, expressing their thoughts and feelings will help them to heal. An example of what you might say is:

CHILD: *'If only I had been a good boy, Daddy would still be alive.'*
PARENT: *'I know you really miss Daddy, darling.'*
CHILD: *'How could Daddy die? I love him so much. I don't understand. Why did it have to happen?'*
PARENT: *'I know you love him, darling, and you want him back so much. Tell me more about how you feel — maybe it will help.'*

Children, like adults, rarely need advice, but they do need love, understanding, and opportunities to express their feelings in their own way, in a safe environment.

Gender differences in grief

By the time we reach adult life, a combination of biology and socialisation ensures that males and females experience and express emotions differently, so it should not come as any great surprise that bereaved males behave very differently to bereaved females. This difference can usually be accommodated by family and friends to some extent when the loss is of an adult relationship — i.e. of a partner, parent, sibling or friend — but can create difficulties in a marital relationship when a child dies.

Universal, internal responses to loss include sadness, pining, and yearning for the lost person or object. These feelings in bereavement are usually passionately intense and their intensity may frighten or overwhelm potential helpers. The bereaved person, afraid of pushing people away and experiencing even more loss, usually adapts their behaviour to make others feel more comfortable. As a general rule, this adapted behaviour in females is more likely to be 'care eliciting', and in males more distancing. Of course there are exceptions, as there are to any generalisations. Some women push people away, expressing their grief outwardly in angry behaviour, while some males cry intensely, which can be equally distancing because it is unfamiliar or doesn't meet others' expectations.

In order to understand this difference, we need to understand biology's contribution to our ability to shed tears. If you are a person who needs accurate information on any subject, it may help to google 'tears', or ask your GP to explain male/female difference from this perspective. We also need to examine the contribution of social conditioning. We are all given gender-specific 'messages' — verbal or implicit — by our families, friends, schools, churches etc. on how we are expected to behave as members of our social group. For example:

Female 'messages' or 'scripting'

- Be sensitive and expressive
- Show feelings (except anger)
- Take care of others — emotionally and physically
- Ventilate/share concerns
- Be domestically competent
- Don't be too competent in other areas
  (don't make men feel threatened)

- Don't be in control (this may be perceived as aggressive)
- Get on with life — put the family first

Male 'messages' or 'scripting'

- Be strong and in control
- Don't show feelings (except anger)
- Feelings are a sign of weakness
- Don't ventilate or share concerns about self
- Be practical
- Take care of others — in a practical sense
- Don't be needy
- Be helpless around domestic tasks
- Get on with life — i.e. work and sport

In some families, females are given messages to encourage behaviour that is socially perceived as masculine. For example — 'In this family we are *all* strong and in control'. Or 'We pride ourselves on not being emotional' or 'We are very private people'. In other families, male children may have emotionally expressive behaviour modelled for them, or rewarded.

Although females are given more social permission to express feelings than males, it is not acceptable even for women to show any emotional intensity which might make others feel uncomfortable or helpless. The same 'rules' apply to dependence and ventilation of concerns. Women are encouraged to be dependent, usually on males, but only to the point where their dependence makes males feel strong, helpful and competent. The degree of emotional dependence which is likely to occur in the acute phase of grief (up to two years) confronts the helplessness in all of us to 'make things better'. Males in particular are likely to respond in these circumstances with behaviour that conveys the message 'get better (or act as if your are) so that I feel useful and can carry out my traditional male role'.

Ventilation of feelings may be acceptable to a degree if the person to whom the woman ventilates is not grieving the same loss. If it is her grieving partner to whom she pours out her concerns and reactions, the very intensity of her reactions, if continued, may threaten the controlled, emotional stance he has adopted in order to feel masculine.

There may be further gender-related complications for a couple when a child dies. Diagram A illustrates the interdependency that develops in an intimate relationship.

Diagram B illustrates the effect on interdependency and intimacy that occurs with the birth of a child.

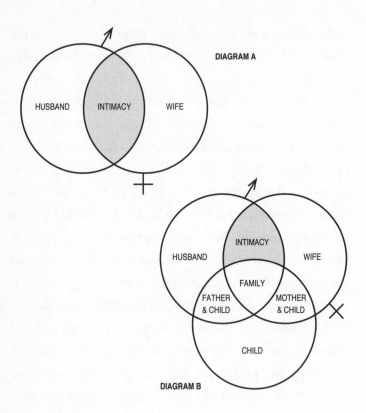

This diagram represents a pronounced change in the distribution of time, energy and focus, to accommodate the emotional and physical needs of the child. Most families accommodate these changes fairly successfully once a routine is established and sleep is restored. In the natural course of events, the situation gradually returns to a version of its original state (or updated version) as the child reaches maturity.

When a woman (or one parent) takes major responsibility for primary parenting needs and the man (or other parent) takes responsibility for primary wage earning, the stay-at-home parent may find their emotional needs being increasingly satisfied by the child, rather than the partner. Children may satisfy that parent's need for touch, love, affection and appreciation, whereas the wage-earning partner may remain dependent on the stay-at-home parent for satisfaction of those needs.

When a child dies, the couple initially mourn the same loss and may express many similar emotions, although the differences explained earlier still exist to some extent.

As time goes on, these differences may become more pronounced. The focus for the wife's grief may remain focused on the child who has died, whereas her partner's grief for the child may decrease in intensity as he (or she) begins to mourn the loss of his partner's emotional (and often physical and sexual) availability. The effect of this difference can be profound on all aspects of the couple's relationship.

Complicated grief

The term 'complicated grief' is used a lot these days, and it is also frequently misused. Grief itself is not complicated, just painful and exhausting. Life is complicated. And people are sometimes complicated.

The term seems to us to imply that there are two kinds of grief — complicated and uncomplicated — which hover like a cloud, waiting to choose someone's shoulders on which to rain. A diagnosis of complicated grief tends to unnecessarily pathologise grief and the grieving person, and could be more sympathetically and accurately stated on health records as 'Jane/Jack is faced with a lot of additional difficulties that are currently complicating her/his grief process.'

Grief is a natural, healthy and painful response to the loss of anyone or anything we value dearly. As mentioned in other parts of this book, we all grieve as we have lived, for a while becoming an exaggerated version of our former selves.

In a safe environment and with the help of compassionate family members, friends, colleagues and neighbours, most of us learn how to live with the pain of loss. The process may be more chaotic, unpredictable and slower than we or other people might have imagined, but, just as a river eventually finds its way to the sea, grief will eventually find its permanent residence in our hearts and minds. Grief cannot be fixed, nor the process shortened. It is what it is. Most of us learn how to live full and rewarding lives, despite the pain that remains with us forever, although in changed form and intensity.

There are certainly things that can complicate the process of accommodating grief. If our earlier life has been complicated, the impact of those events may 'bleed into the present'. If our present environment is unsafe, grief is likely to feel unsafe. If we have to deal with concurrent problems — such as job loss, financial difficulties or the need to move home, school or country — when we are still raw and vulnerable, our distress level will understandably be higher. If we lack family and social support, our distress is likely to be exacerbated. It is the other things impacting on our grief that cause the problem, not grief itself. Grief is not a problem to be solved; it is the effect of a significant loss on every part of our being. No matter how much we may have anticipated a death and believe that we are well prepared, when someone we love dies it may still feel sudden, and our emotional and physical reactions may surprise us. Grief is painful and exhausting enough already, without the addition of life's problems.

Let's look at an example of grief that is uncomplicated by life.

Mavis and Jack were happily married for 40 years when Jack was diagnosed with cancer of the bowel. He had surgery and chemotherapy and appeared to be recovering well. They decided to celebrate with the river cruise in Europe that they'd planned to take after retirement. The trip was all they had hoped. A couple of months after their return, metastases were found in Jack's liver and lungs. He died at home three months later, surrounded by family — Mavis, daughters Anna and Julie, son Matt, their partners and the six grandchildren Jack adored. Support from the local palliative care team ensured that Jack's death was peaceful and pain-free. Mavis saw a bereavement counsellor five weeks after Jack's death because her children were concerned that she cried every day and was postponing her return to bowls. Her bereavement counsellor found nothing in her history to warrant concern. She was just passionately sad, which was understandable given the circumstances.

Mavis had grown up in a happy family, married for love, had the children she wanted, enjoyed family and social life and had no current financial worries. Life had been pretty good overall, with the usual ups and downs of living. Taking time out to 'lick her wounds' and regather her resources was the way she had always dealt with rough patches, so her counsellor was able to reassure her children that all she needed was time, loving support and a few strategies to help her manage her responses. She would see her counsellor for sessions periodically.

Ray's story, on the other hand, is a good example of a complicated life and its impact on grief.

Ray's wife Betty died in a car accident, killed by a drunk driver. His GP referred him for counselling because he seemed angry and was drinking heavily in the evenings. History taking revealed that he had been happily married for 20 years but by choice had no children. Regular social drinking was part of their lifestyle, but neither partner drank to excess. Ray's early life was complex and difficult. He was placed in foster care at the age of five when FACS removed him and his two siblings from their home because of parental alcoholism and physical abuse. He remained in a foster home with his siblings for two years, but he became separated from them when the two younger children (aged four and three) were adopted. He saw them occasionally until they were adults but later lost touch with them when they married and moved overseas. Ray was a builder's labourer and enjoyed the physical work and the companionship of his mates — three men who had worked with him on many occasions. They drank together at the end of the day, but the other men had wives and families and were more temperate in their alcohol use. They were concerned about Ray. Ray's counsellor decided that teamwork was necessary.

After a few individual sessions, where Ray was able to talk with the counsellor about Betty, their relationship and the difficulties he was now experiencing, Ray gave the counsellor permission to invite his three mates to a group session. Together they developed a way of structuring time so that Ray was occupied doing things that he enjoyed and minimised time alone. Loneliness was part of his history and, in the past, had contributed to him getting into trouble with the law. He wanted to honour his wife by staying 'on the straight and narrow' and needed his mates' help to do so. They were very willing, and their wives were supportive. His friends genuinely cared about him, a big plus in the equation. Ray made good progress and, into the second year after Betty's death, his drinking was under control and the energy in his anger was also reduced and redirected. He was then referred to a psychotherapist who also specialised in bereavement counselling, so that the grief of his early life and other issues from that time could be addressed appropriately.

Ray's grief for Betty was straightforward. He simply loved and missed her. His early life, on the other hand, was very complicated and was certainly 'bleeding into the present'.

If our early life has been complicated by neglect, abuse, mental illness, alcohol or other drug dependence, many changes of home or school, bereavement at a young age, poverty, intense loneliness or any other distressing life event, our reactions and responses to a recent bereavement may be unusually intense or prolonged. We need to be cautious here about how we define 'intense' or 'prolonged'. Remember, we grieve as we have lived, so what appears to be unusually intense or prolonged for one person may be normal for another.

It is hard for anyone to provide help, or to assist us to access appropriate help, unless they know our history and understand all that we are and are capable of being. Good teamwork seems to be the most effective way of helping most of us, and this becomes increasingly important if we have faced many difficulties in our life.

Talking to children about traumatic death

Imparting the news

Having a discussion with children about the death of someone important to them is never easy. Ideally, children are best informed about a death by someone with whom they don't have an ongoing, significant relationship. This is because of our tendency, no matter what our age, to 'behead the messenger'. It helps if parents or other caregivers can be with the child or young person to provide safety and comfort while a doctor, police officer or other professional person delivers the news. But life does not always provide ideal circumstances, and we all just do the best we can at the time.

When the news involves telling a child that the person died as a result of suicide, the task may seem even more daunting — especially if the adult conveying the news is grieving the same death. The word 'suicide' seems to stimulate strong reactions in most people, reactions that may be exacerbated by media attention and the current focus on suicide prevention programs. The message many people receive is that death from suicide is somehow worse than death from other causes. Initially, the manner of death may be in the foreground, especially if we were present at the death or found the body of the person who died. However, no matter how someone we love dies, in the long-term it is their physical absence that causes most pain and distress.

Before we talk to children about suicide, we need to have time to process our own thoughts and feelings. If our anxiety is intense, we may need to ask ourselves a few questions. Is our reaction because we have previously experienced the suicide death of someone we love, and this recent death is bringing all of those feelings back into the foreground again? Is it because we've had suicidal thoughts ourselves and feel guilty? Is it because we blame ourselves for the death or believe we could have prevented it? Do we think the death is someone else's fault and feel angry?

If the answers to these questions are hard to process, it may help to talk to someone we trust and respect before speaking to children in our care.

The best time to talk about suicide

As with any conversation about death, the best time to talk about it is before children and young people are personally affected. If they hear the word 'suicide' and ask what it means, it is best not to react emotionally. Take time to sit with them and ask them what they think it means. Their answer will provide cues for how to proceed.

Overall, they need simple facts. If you are in a position to have this discussion with a young child before a death has occurred, you might begin by asking them how many ways they know that a person may die. It's useful to do this as a pen-and-paper exercise or, even better, on a whiteboard. This process helps to make the discussion a little more objective and gives the child a feeling of control. Do the exercise with them. When you have made a reasonable list, add the word 'suicide' if it hasn't already been included. Ask if they know what suicide means. If they don't, explain that when people choose to end their own lives, we call that suicide. If they already know what it means, or after you have posed the previous question, ask them to imagine what might make someone choose to end their life.

When you have heard their answer, explain that

even if someone is depressed, very worried about something or in a lot of physical pain, there are usually other ways to make themselves feel better. Ask if they know what those might be. Explain that someone who is depressed enough to end their life is what we might call 'sick in their thinking'. They may not be able to make good decisions at that time. Encourage the child to make a list of trusted people they could talk to if they were worried. Explain that talking to someone is a brave and healthy thing to do, and better than keeping worried, scared or sad feelings inside.

When a child is bereaved as a result of suicide

Children do best in the long-term when they have access to truth and are included in whatever is happening within the family. Although they should hear the truth, they should never be brutalised by being given information in harsh or very graphic language. What they need to know is that adults who care about them will answer their questions and give them information as they need it.

As already stated, it is best if a person NOT in an ongoing relationship with the child is the 'bearer of bad tidings'. A professional or someone not affected by the death is the best person to tell the child what has happened, as long as there is a person present that the child trusts and who can provide comfort.

Make sure the child is in a safe place where they feel as if they have some degree of control, perhaps holding a toy or pet that gives them comfort. Begin by asking what the child knows about what has happened. The next step will be indicated by their response. You can use what we said in the previous section as a guideline for explaining if they need simple facts, and you can correct any misinformation they may have. Keep it as simple and unemotional as possible. Try not to make suicide sound more frightening than death from any other cause.

Tell them what will happen next, and assure them that they can ask anything and you will either answer their questions or find someone who can. As soon as possible after your conversation, help the child find something practical and physical to do. Make sure they have access to paper, pens, crayons, clay or other familiar materials for expressing feelings. Some children, especially boys, might prefer to do something more active such as kicking a ball around.

As they grieve, children — like adults — will become an exaggerated version of what they were before the death occurred. If their behaviour concerns you, or you need strategies to help them on a day-to-day basis, contact The National Centre for Childhood Grief, known as 'A Friend's Place'. You can ask them to send you pamphlets, a CD and/ or a book list, or you can talk to a counsellor. There are lots of resources available to help you. Their phone number is 1300 654 556, their email address is info@childhoodgrief.org.au and their website is www.childhoodgrief.org.au. The centre also provides an outreach email service: afriendsplace@me.org.au.

When a child is bereaved as a result of homicide

The guidelines above are a starting point, but because homicide often occurs within a family setting or may have been witnessed by the child, it is usually best to seek outside help. Children are likely to suffer from anxiety if the perpetrator hasn't been jailed, and they will need lots of reassurance as well as practical changes around the home to increase their feelings of safety.

For guidelines related to your specific situation, contact The National Centre for Childhood Grief (refer to the information above) or the Homicide

Victims' Support Group on 1800 191 777 or info@
hvsgnsw.org.au.

When a child is bereaved
as a result of a natural disaster

If a child has been personally affected or bereaved
as a result of a natural disaster, it is best to keep
them with you as you and others who are affected
participate in debriefing. Being together is helpful
for most people, so that experiences can be shared
without inhibition or judgement. Whatever you,
as the adult, need at this time (as long as it isn't
harmful, such as numbing pain with alcohol or other
drugs) is likely to be what the child or children need
as well. If you are concerned about your own or your
children's reactions in the long-term, contact the
resources already given in this chapter.

If the child has NOT been bereaved in these
circumstances, it is easier to make the discussion more
objective and factual. A pen-and-paper or whiteboard
exercise can help children talk about and make a list
of all the things in their life that they can control,
or that their family can control. Then make a list of
what can't be controlled — for example, the weather.
Discuss what we can all do to make ourselves as safe as

possible in circumstances we can't control, and what we might do in an emergency.

Children often feel braver when they have thought ahead and know what to do to help someone or something else. For example, you might discuss how they could help a pet feel safe in an electrical storm or when there are fireworks around. Have a family escape plan in case of a house fire or flood that includes what to do for pets. It's important to find out what makes each child feel safe.

Don't allow children to watch replays of natural or other disasters. They should know what is happening in their world (as they need access to truth and inclusion), but once is enough. Always make sure they are distracted after hearing or seeing a scene that is traumatic by doing something active, practical or fun, or all of these combined. Sensitive children may benefit from writing to those affected or sending small gifts — anything that helps them to feel useful, rather than helpless and out of control.

When a child is bereaved as a result of an act of terror

Talking to children about acts of terror is much the same as talking to them about any other distressing event: they need access to truthful information, which is given to them as calmly as possible; they need time to express their reactions; and they need opportunities to ask questions. Once questions have been answered, they need to be distracted from worrying. Physical activity that uses adrenalin — particularly if the activity is fun — is usually most helpful. Later, in preparation for sleep, they should be reassured about their safety. Tell them about the measures being taken by people in authority to keep everyone safe, and reassure them about the safety of their neighbourhood, their home, their bedroom and their family. Explain the difference between vigilance and paranoia in clear and simple language.

Acts of terror are not as frequent as news reports might have us believe, but when they do occur, they are certainly distressing. Our current ability to transmit news instantly and dramatically has made us all part of a global community where it is harder to turn a blind eye to the suffering of others. Each time an act of terror is reported, we are likely to feel an increase in our own heart rate; by the time we have heard and seen numerous replays of the event, we may feel like we are caught up in a global wave of anxiety that can easily become an emotional tsunami.

When vulnerable children see, hear and feel the anxiety of the adults around them, and see multiple replays of terrorist events on television, their anxiety can increase even more rapidly than that of adults. They may have difficulty going to sleep, experience nightmares or become afraid of being alone. Ideally, children should watch news items about terrorism in the company of trusted adults. If the distressing event has not directly impacted on them, then children should only be exposed to it once.

These events provide an opportunity to teach children that it is important to care for the distress of others and do what is possible to help. Distract the children by focusing on what remedial action or change is achievable in the context of their own lives. To feel helpless in the face of another's pain is empathic; relentless focus on helplessness is disempowering.

Whenever children demonstrate empathy, help them to *do* something — however small and simple — that has an achievable and observable outcome. For example, they could send letters, cards or gifts to children and adults directly affected by acts of terror; they could write to politicians; or they could pen a story for their local paper or school magazine. Feelings expressed in constructive action can act as an invaluable antidote to fear.

After the initial shock

Bereavement and its possible consequences

The shock of bereavement has an effect on the pituitary gland — a pea-sized gland which sits at the base of the brain and secretes a hormone known as ACTH. This hormone is the chemical which helps produce the adrenalin that regulates the fight-or-flight response. Coupled with the production of adrenalin is the production of cortizole (similar to cortisone) — an immunosuppressant which decreases the production of T-lymphocytes, our surveillance cells; they are responsible for keeping infection and other abnormal cells under control. When T-lymphocytes are depleted, for any reason, we are said to be immuno-suppressed. If we are unable to fight off infection or control abnormal cells, viruses and bacteria in our bodies now have free rein, making us vulnerable to colds, influenza, cold sores, upper respiratory or urinary tract infections, boils, conjunctivitis and so on. If our bodies are not quickly returned to normal, we are also at risk of developing more serious health problems. Some studies of bereaved women in North America, for example, have demonstrated that they are more vulnerable to serious illness and premature death than their non-bereaved counterparts.

As strange as it may seem, shedding tears of grief can actually help to reduce our vulnerability to infection because our tears contain healing and sedating chemicals.

Alcohol and other drug use

Most newly bereaved people find that their intake of alcohol and other drugs (such as nicotine, caffeine, analgesics, tranquillisers) increases, usually on a temporary basis. The pain of grief can be so intense that most of us would do anything to anaesthetise feelings. We may ask our doctor to help, or be encouraged by others to do so, and be prescribed tranquillisers or sleeping tablets, or both.

Sleeping tablets occasionally, or a tranquilliser at times of panic, may help a bereaved person regain a feeling of control of their grief, rather than it continuing to control them. Used in this way drugs can be helpful, but prolonged use can delay grief and readily lead to tolerance and then dependence. The last thing a bereaved person needs is another problem to deal with.

On occasions, people are prescribed anti-depressants a few weeks after the death of someone they love, when their passionate sadness is incorrectly diagnosed as depression. In our long experience in working with bereaved people of all ages and cultures, it is most unlikely that anyone who hasn't suffered a depressive illness in the past will develop one as the result of a single event such as bereavement.

However, if depression existed in the past, then symptoms may worsen in acute grief and may require the attention of the bereaved person's medical practitioner and/or counsellor. Sometimes current grief may re-stimulate experiences from the past, particularly those that did not receive adequate or appropriate attention, and in so doing, create complications that indicate the need for professional help.

If anything about your grief concerns you, including the way you use drugs of any kind to lessen pain, don't hesitate to see a skilled professional. People who understand grief will not judge your behaviour.

More usually, most of us end up feeling as if we are

drowning in tea or coffee as helpers struggle to feel useful. Each new visitor may put the kettle on for a cup of tea or percolate a strong brew of coffee. By the end of the day we may have overdosed on caffeine, and our resultant agitation is easily interpreted as panic. Further, the impending sense of doom that high levels of caffeine can create may then tempt us to treat the symptoms with alcohol or tranquillisers, especially if the panic occurs at bed time and we are unable to sleep. We are better off in the long term if we withdraw from caffeine, and 'treat' our agitation by doing something to use up energy. Tidy the house, clean the garage, bathe the dog, mow the lawn or do the ironing — tasks that can leave us feeling tired and virtuous rather than anxious.

Relationships

The crisis of bereavement, like any major life crisis, frequently results in review and changes in relationships. We all remember the saying 'you can tell who your real friends are when you're in crisis'. Your perspective on life and your priorities change; things that previously seemed important may no longer interest you; acquaintances may fall by the wayside; complex relationships which are characterised by conflict or unreasonable demands are no longer worth the effort. Bereavement can provide an opportunity for a 'clean sweep', a chance to start over, to do the things that are really important to you, to spend time with people who really count. When we are confronted with the finiteness of life, we know to our core that life is precious, and that no matter how long we may have, time is too precious to be wasted.

However, a word of caution. Before making any radical changes, it is good to remind ourselves that it is us, the bereaved, who have changed, not the other or others.

Many bereaved people find that it is important to make new friends — as well as retaining old, tried-and-trusted friends. New friends get to know you as you are now, with no expectations or hopes that you will return to being your former self.

Bereavement changes us all in some way, and for many the changes can be positive, allowing us to be more, not less of who we really are. Many of us will become more assertive, less inhibited, more outspoken about our thoughts and feelings, more prone to taking risks. Radical changes tend to occur while we are still in the 'what have I got to lose?' phase, when the pain of grief numbs our concerns about what others may think. These changes may be welcomed by some, and distress others. A true friend, one who is 'you centred', or an objective outsider, may give you constructive feedback about any changes so that you don't have to be afraid about venturing too far out 'into left field', or of losing people who may later be important to you.

Some changes in relationship may concern you. For example, your relationship with a partner, children or parents may be temporarily affected because you are unable to fulfil the role you previously played. Your resources may be depleted so that you have a reduced ability to be other centred. With patience and understanding, most of these relationships will eventually return to a point of equilibrium, but if you become concerned, or are in danger of impulsively ending a previously valued relationship, a 'check-up' with a skilled bereavement counsellor may be a good idea.

Not all bereaved people are able to make changes they think are positive or necessary for their wellbeing. As previously mentioned, most grieving people spend a lot of time and energy trying to make others feel more comfortable, and in so doing, sacrifice their own needs. Grief makes many of us feel regressed and dependent, and afraid of losing the relationships we still have. If we have previously been somewhat compliant, peacemakers afraid of rocking the boat, we may become more so in grief, and feel resentful in the process. If your compliant behaviour continues to distress you, ask a friend to support you in making changes, or seek the help of a bereavement counsellor.

Sexuality and grief

As mentioned earlier in this book, grief affects all parts of our being. The behaviour that accompanies that effect is determined by many factors, including gender, age, physical and mental health, and the environment in which we grieve. Biology and socialisation influence the stimuli that enhance and diminish libido or sexual interest and expression. Women's biology and socialisation are more likely to encourage them to achieve and desire intimacy via verbal communication, sensitivity and affection. Men, on the other hand, also because of biology and socialisation, may be left with the belief that intimacy can only be achieved through sex.

Most people's sexual responses are affected by acute grief. Both men and women may lose interest altogether for a time, and even those males who remain interested may find their performance affected. Temporary impotence or premature ejaculation is not uncommon. For others, desire may increase rather than decrease, as they seek comfort, reassurance, warmth and distraction from emotional pain. These changes and differences can usually be accommodated within a relationship when the loss is not experienced to the same degree by both partners — for example, when the parent of one of the partners dies. In that case, one may be able to provide enough nurture and understanding for the other to allow intense grief to heal sufficiently for equilibrium to return to the relationship in a relatively short period of time.

When a child dies, however, neither partner has enough resources to provide adequate nurture for the other. In addition, each partner is likely to need care and comfort in a different way, and may interpret the other's needs as strange or abnormal. For example, if the male seeks comfort through sex, and his partner feels physically and emotionally incapable of responding, they may each withdraw, feeling rejected or misunderstood, and critical of the other. She may see him as selfish and demanding, and he may see her as frigid and withholding. At times, in a conscious or unconscious attempt to avoid pain, one or both of them may have some anxieties about resuming a sexual relationship. After all, their sexual relationship produced the child they now mourn. Why risk another hurt?

When a child dies, women often feel guilty, in some way responsible, whereas men may feel angry and blame someone else. The man's anger may push his wife away, particularly when her needs are for gentleness, comfort and reassurance, and her subsequent withdrawal may make him feel rejected. It is easy in these circumstances to create a vicious circle which serves to distance them from each other. If the distance becomes too great it is easy to fear that the relationship might come to an end, just when each partner needs it most.

As distressing as it might feel, distancing can also serve a positive function for a grieving couple. In grief we all regress, that is, feel much younger on the inside than our chronological age. Regression makes us feel vulnerable, at times incompetent, and we tend to lose self-esteem as a result. Most bereaved people when asked say that they feel somewhere between eight and fifteen. Those who experienced grief or trauma very early in their lives may regress to that internal feeling memory, and experience even more vulnerability. If we allow ourselves to examine this situation objectively for a moment and imagine the relationship dynamic of two eight- to fifteen-year-olds, it is understandable why they might experience difficulties in the early months of grief — sometimes until the third year. Eight- to fifteen-year-olds shouldn't be married.

It is important that caring relatives and friends, or perhaps a bereavement counsellor, help to 'hold' the relationship by caring for each individual separately instead of forcing them to focus on their relationship while their resources are depleted. We, as a caring community, should ideally take care of their different needs until they are sufficiently familiar with their grief to feel more in control of their thoughts, feelings and behaviour. In this way, we can all help to minimise damage to important relationships.

When both partners are eventually able to understand that interest or disinterest is neither good nor bad, it 'just is', they may be able to begin a conversation that decreases distance. Both partners are seeking comfort in their own way, struggling to survive, and with the help of a supportive outsider, may be able to learn ways of meeting some of their own needs so that they don't place unrealistic demands on a relationship with depleted resources. As abhorrent as clichés tend to be, time usually does help in this situation, along with patience, understanding and a lot of external nurture and support.

If a couple's sexual relationship remains out of balance for a prolonged period or begins to cause either partner unnecessary distress, it is best to seek professional counselling, preferably from someone who understands both relationships and grief.

Sexual 'acting out'

Many people 'act out' sexually when someone close to them is dying, or when they are newly bereaved. Although this is usually a temporary phenomenon, often a once-only occurrence, the behaviour may shock the grieving person as well as others close to them. Guilt and remorse may follow, with the grieving person asking themself, 'How could I do it, how could I be so selfish, how could I do something that would normally offend my morals and ethics?' There are many possible explanations, and the behaviour appears to be common.

Sometimes it is just the need to be held, for others it may be a reaction to the fear of death (libido = life force or energy — the antithesis of death). If this has been part of your own experience, it is important to understand your behaviour, to mentally say 'sorry' if that seems necessary, to forgive yourself instead of self-flagellating. If, after finding an explanation for your own behaviour, you are still unable to move on, talk to a trained bereavement counsellor so that you can gain a more objective perspective.

Being supportive

The support team: family, friends, colleagues, professional carers

It is important for support people to understand their own responses to dying, death and bereavement before they can help anyone else. Self-awareness is invaluable. Carers should not be afraid of intimacy or passion, but should have a clear sense of boundaries and ethics so that they don't exploit the vulnerability of bereaved people.

It is important too that we resist any temptation to impose our beliefs or consciously or unconsciously prevent bereaved people from doing what is in their best interests. For example, if we aren't convinced of the benefits of spending time with the body of the deceased, we may convey this in our manner and discourage the bereaved person from participating in what could be a most helpful experience.

Supporting someone experiencing shock and denial

We have already talked about the initial reactions bereaved people usually feel when they first learn of the death of someone they love. Shock jumbles thoughts and stimulates defensive responses like 'No! No! No! It's not true'. This is part of the emotional filter system our bodies provide to allow small amounts of information to penetrate at a rate we can handle. There may be little overt arousal and the bereaved person may seem stunned.

As care-givers, we usually feel helpless at this time. Helplessness is a form of empathy, not an indication of uselessness. The bereaved person also feels helpless, so our helplessness may for a little while enable us to stand beside them with compassionate understanding. One of the most important things we can do as supporters is to just *be* there, be totally present with all aspects of our being. Don't try to make yourself feel better by offering platitudes or clichés — just try to accept the situation for a moment — because it is not possible to fix anything, or to offer anything significant that can prevent or reduce pain.

If you are familiar with the bereaved person, if intimacy and closeness have existed before in your relationship, then touching may be helpful and reassuring. However, without that relationship history, touch may feel like an intrusion, an attempt to make the carer feel better when they don't know what else to do. Touch can be interpreted as a non-verbal platitude — a kind of 'there, there dear, everything will be alright' response.

Creating safety, attending to any necessary physical needs, gentle reassurance, the ability to listen and attention to practical needs are all that is necessary.

Supporting someone experiencing disorientation

Newly bereaved people often feel disoriented in relation to time, place and person. In an effort to block reality, they may not remember what is happening, what you ask, or who asked the question. They may miss or forget details in important conversations and need you to remember for them. Forgetfulness and being unfocused is part of the body's way of recoiling after shock.

Provide an environment where it is permissible to protest and express feelings. Be patient. Don't rush. Fine details should not matter at this time so allow room for error, for mishearing, for 'muddleheadedness'. Allow the bereaved to talk, as much as they want, no matter how rambling their thoughts may sound. Hearing themselves speak out loud may help them to organise their thinking and allow more reality to sink in. As this occurs, feelings may intensify and be overtly expressed. All you have to do is keep them safe.

Supporting someone experiencing anger

Anger may range from mild frustration to intense rage, although rage is rare in our experience. Previously angry people may become more so at this time, but grief doesn't turn a previously gentle person into someone whose rage is to be feared. Bereaved people may need permission to express their anger because their anger frightens them or others who then try to inhibit their behaviour. The most effective and powerful form of permission is to just allow what is, without appearing to disapprove. You don't need to give people verbal permission.

Children also need to be able to express anger. They may act out, displaying destructive behaviour that is unusual for them, breaking toys, injuring dolls, or hitting other children. Anger that doesn't cause harm to self, others or valuable possessions is fine, but clear boundaries need to be put in place (for adults as well as children) if aggressive behaviour continues. As explained before, grief is an explanation, not an excuse for aggression. The child (or adult) may feel out of control, as if life is out of control, and in their regressed state, be unconsciously asking for someone to let them know where the boundaries are.

Finally, resist any temptation to force expressions of anger where anger doesn't exist. Contrary to popular belief, *à la* 'stage theories of grief', not everyone experiences anger. Some people only ever feel sad or afraid.

As already mentioned, the best help that carers can provide is to keep the situation safe and allow the bereaved to say and do what is important for them. Bottling up anger to please others can be destructive to health in the long term. It can also be destructive for helpers to encourage the bereaved to express anger over and over, bashing the stuffing out of a pillow, or ripping up a telephone book in the misguided belief that this activity, dramatic as it may appear, will get rid of 'it'. What this exercise is likely to do is help the carer to feel better because they are doing something, while increasing the 'anger muscle' in the bereaved.

Initially, all you have to do is be passive, allowing what occurs naturally to be expressed, without judgement. Anger is part of survival, and may provide the energy the bereaved person needs to keep them going.

It is important to contain and control anger that becomes destructive to self or others, and when doing so, take responsibility for your actions by telling the truth — i.e. 'I can't let you do this' or 'It distresses me to see you doing this' rather than 'I am doing this for your own good', which can sound patronising.

Supporting someone experiencing guilt

A pinch of guilt is a necessary part of our socialisation, and one of the ways we learn right from wrong. We know that people unable to feel guilt or remorse have serious personality disorders. If people do us wrong, we may want them to feel guilty and to demonstrate genuine remorse before we can forgive their behaviour. We know too, that too much guilt, especially in our early developmental years, may leave us with a lifelong problem that inhibits our ability to live life fully. There seems to be a line somewhere in between extremes that makes us and our society feel comfortable.

Guilt in grief tends to make others feel uncomfortable, usually because of its intensity, a kind of stepping over that invisible middle line. It is often expressed as a lament, pleading, a necessary ventilation of intense emotion — of great sorrow. Our bodies may bend over, it is difficult to make eye contact, our verbal expression usually a dialogue with self and the universe. We may use words like 'It's all my fault', 'I shouldn't have…' or 'Why didn't I…?' — all expressions of love and anguish. What we are really saying is 'I feel *so* bad, *so* responsible…can anybody hear me?'

Guilt seems to be one of the hardest aspects of grief for supporters to tolerate. There is a great temptation to rush in with reassurances like 'You mustn't blame yourself', 'It wasn't your fault', 'You couldn't have stopped/prevented…', 'Any of us would/could have done that…'.

Bereaved people expressing guilt do not need anyone to 'fix things', to correct irrational thoughts with factual information, or to placate by passing tissues, or attempting to hug or hold. What they do need is someone who has the courage to listen, to hear how awful it is to feel responsible, to believe there is something that might have been done to prevent the death, if only… They need supportive people to be there, knowing that the bereaved person is expressing in their guilt 'I love this person so much that there isn't anything I wouldn't have done to prevent their death'.

As helpers, we may fear that by our silence or passivity we are confirming that the person *is* responsible, and sometimes they are. For example, if I run over my child, leave them unattended near deep water etc., I am responsible. But whether or not guilt is based on fact, the grieving person simply needs us to hear the depth of their anguish, to acknowledge that we can hear, without being overwhelmed by our own discomfort. We could say something self-disclosing like 'I can't begin to imagine how awful it might be to love someone so much and feel responsible for their death. Tell me more about what makes you feel responsible'.

Listening with compassion is particularly important in the early days and weeks. Later, when intensity subsides a little, we may be able to correct misinformation that is causing unnecessary anguish. We may be able to ask the right questions at the right time, and occasionally add our perception of the event from a different vantage point.

Bereaved people may express guilt about the death forever, whenever they think about it, and that is OK.

It is simply the intensity of feeling that changes, not the words.

Supporting someone experiencing depression, sadness, loneliness

Once the funeral is over and friends and relatives have gone back to their normal lives, the body's biochemistry begins to allow the reality and foreverness of death to penetrate more deeply. Bereaved people often begin to experience extreme tiredness, lethargy, or feelings of hopelessness and loneliness. As mentioned before, it is easy for bereaved people, and their supporters, to interpret these reactions as 'getting worse', 'going downhill', 'going mad' or depression. Supporters may feel guilty for abandoning them and encourage visits to a doctor for medication, often in an attempt to assuage their guilt. Sadness and loneliness are painfully real — not illnesses that can be cured. It is hard enough to survive from day to day, let alone imagining weeks, months, years — a lifetime of having to live in this state. Anguish and fear can stimulate thoughts like 'I wish I didn't have to wake up in the morning', or 'If it weren't for the children/my parents/my work etc., I'd kill myself'.

The loneliness of grief is hard to describe — a feeling that seems to go to the very core of our being. As hard as it might be to imagine, the intensity and constancy of these feelings will not last forever. Grief *will* change — not be 'cured'. Most bereaved people learn how to live with 'it' if they receive the right kind of help.

Teamwork is needed from this point, because no one person can meet all the needs of someone who is passionately sad. Those who care could phone, write, send frequent emails, or work out a roster for helping with practical tasks. It is important for supporters not to lock themselves into a predictable pattern, for example, by phoning every day or week at the same time. Life may make it impossible to meet rigid commitments, and what is too predictable often loses value. What bereaved people need to be able to count on is that others care, and won't disappear.

It helps if support people remember times that may be particularly difficult — sunset, weekends, particularly Sundays when non-bereaved people are usually off doing family or couple things. Birthdays, anniversaries, other special occasions and celebratory times can also be particularly difficult. Drop in sometimes for a 'cuppa', and ask questions about the person who is grieving and the dead person. Bring them back 'into life', keep them alive by talking about them, and asking about the bereaved person's relationship with them. Don't be afraid of your questions stimulating tears — tears are more likely to help than hinder.

One of the hardest things for most bereaved people is having others avoid mentioning the person who has died — acting as if they never existed. Where children are involved, it is important for them to witness the fact that people can remain as important to us in death as they are in life. In this way, children are reassured that if they die, they will never lose their place in people's hearts and minds.

The acute phase of grief lasts for months, often up to two years. When we are grieving a relationship that is central to our lives, to our sense of identity, it can take up to five to six years to learn to find comparable meaning again in life, to fully accommodate the experience. This is not meant to frighten anyone who is newly bereaved, or imply that grief will consume your being 24/7 for five years. It is simply acknowledging that it takes a long time to reorganise a world that has been changed forever.

Helpful and unhelpful comments and questions

What do I say?

The majority of people find it difficult to speak to a newly bereaved person and struggle to find the right words. While there are no perfect words, you need to be supportive, sympathetic and respectful with what you say. Struggling to convey the right sentiment may feel uncomfortable, but that is not a good reason to avoid contact with a bereaved person, who may be feeling lonely and vulnerable. In fact, the struggle may be an indication of sensitivity and compassion. We aren't meant to feel comfortable in the face of another person's emotional or physical pain, and most of us initially feel helpless. We need to remind ourselves that feeling helpless is different to being useless.

Helpful comments

Telling our truth is important; the way in which we tell our truth is even more so. It's important to establish a personal connection with the bereaved person by expressing heartfelt sympathy and sorrow. We may begin with a version of 'I was shocked/saddened to hear of your husband's death, and I really wish there was something wise I could say or some helpful thing I could do to make you feel better. But I know that's not possible. All I can really do at this moment is care. I'll put some thought into what I could offer in the long-term and get back to you.'

Don't make promises you can't keep. If you say you'll get back to them, make sure you do. There are so many things that we can offer in the long-term, depending on our own circumstances, of course. We can deliver meals, provide transport, help with the garden, take children to school or sporting activities, pop in for coffee and a chat, email and send cards from time to time expressing thoughts and wishes. We can invite bereaved individuals and families to social activities — as long as we are able to accept a refusal without taking it personally.

We may acknowledge something we loved or appreciated about the person who died, and what we will miss. The comment might be as simple as 'Every time I walked past your house and your husband/wife was working in the garden, they had a friendly word or infectious smile that brightened my day. I'll miss that connection, so I can only begin to imagine all the things you'll miss.'

Whenever we express appreciation of the person who died and mention missing them, it's important to acknowledge the fact that our loss is only a fraction of what the bereaved person is likely to feel. We need to remind ourselves that we are not the chief mourner.

Unhelpful comments

When we think of annoying or unhelpful comments made to bereaved people, clichés come to mind first. Clichés are familiar to most of us and can be annoying at any time, but they are even more so when we are made hypersensitive by grief. Examples of annoying clichés (some mentioned earlier in this book) are:

- 'You mustn't blame yourself.'
- 'He wouldn't want you to be upset.'
- 'You're young enough to get married again.'
- 'You're lucky that you have other children.'
- 'You're young enough to have another baby.'
- 'He's at peace now.'

- Any comment that begins with 'oh well'. For example: 'Oh well, she had a good innings.'

Other comments to avoid are those that contain 'must' or 'should' — a prescription for how we think the person should feel, think or be. For example: 'You must feel angry/guilty/frustrated', 'you must remember that there's still lots to look forward to' and 'you should think of the kids'. Many bereaved people say that they could write a book about all the hurtful, insensitive or unhelpful comments showered on them when they were feeling vulnerable.

Clichés and other throwaway lines are designed to make us, the speaker, feel better, not the bereaved person. They allow us to delude ourselves that we've given a helpful pep talk and done our duty. Insensitive offhand lines also provide an opportunity for a quick escape. The bereaved person has no escape — they have to live with their distress 24 hours a day. The very least we can do is have the courage to stay still for a while and listen empathically.

Finally, telling the bereaved person to 'let me know if there is anything I can do to help', no matter how genuine, is not helpful. Most bereaved people can't think clearly enough in the early days, weeks and months to be able to formulate a request. It is best to let them know what you can offer — preferably in writing — so they can refer back to and follow up on your offer.

Helpful questions

Don't be afraid to ask questions. Whether we ask questions or make comments, it's always possible that the bereaved person will cry. We need to remind ourselves that it is unlikely that we have caused the tears — we have simply provided an opportunity for them to be expressed. Let the person cry and encourage them to talk through their tears, but don't pass the tissues. Giving the bereaved person tissues is an unspoken message that you want them to stop crying — but crying might be the most helpful thing they can do at that moment.

Examples of helpful questions are:

- 'What part of the day is hardest for you?'
- 'What practical things are you finding difficult at the moment?'
- 'What is the most helpful thing I could do for you and/or your family at the moment?'

If the person answers the last question with 'I don't know', this will let you know that they're feeling regressed and unable to think clearly. You could then respond with a version of 'Okay. I'll have a think about it and get back to you. If I offer to do something and it doesn't feel right, don't hesitate to say so. I won't be offended.'

Before you visit a bereaved person, you might ask 'Is there a good time for me to call in?' If you are visiting a bereaved person, but it is obvious that your presence is undesired at that moment, it is prudent to ask 'Is there a better time for me to call in to see how you're doing?'

Unhelpful questions

Any questions designed to satisfy our curiosity are unhelpful. The same questions, asked due to genuine concern, can have the opposite effect. The nature of your relationship with the bereaved person will determine what is likely to be helpful or unhelpful, as long as you remember that bereaved people become an exaggerated version of what they were before the death, and regression will make them use old, familiar coping strategies. If they were very independent, or very private, they are likely to become more so. They may reject offers of help or resent what may feel like intrusive questions until they are feeling less raw and more in control of their thoughts and feelings.

If in doubt about what to say, you can always use the email support service mentioned on page 130 — afriendsplace@me.org.au — to ask for suggestions.

Accommodating loss

Beginning to reorganise life

This period is marked by a gradually increasing ability to think clearly and logically, establish a new routine, and make plans for the future, even if the future simply means next week. Being able to acknowledge that there is a future is a big step. There may be many practical problems to address — finances, hospital and medical bills, schooling, housing, running a home and all its attendant chores. Difficulties are often of a practical nature, made more complex because of reduced energy and difficulties in retaining information. Memory loss is common and many people find it hard to read books in the first year. Children may struggle to concentrate at school. Equilibrium will be restored in time, usually into the second year, but if not, it can help to see a competent bereavement counsellor for a 'check-up'.

Retaining social connection is vital, and usually involves a need to pretend, to act 'as if'. Accept as many invitations to do things with others as you are able, and act 'as if' you are enjoying yourself. Little by little, small bubbles of pleasure will surface, even if short lived. Guilt may return when you find yourself laughing for a moment, or having a good time, then suddenly remembering the person who has died. People often punish themselves by saying and thinking words like 'How can I laugh when X is dead? Does this mean I don't really feel very much, that I didn't love them as much as I believed? Am I shallow and selfish?' At these times, bereaved people often long to feel intense pain again to reassure themselves of their connection with the person they love.

Illusions can also create distress. You may be in a crowded social situation, a supermarket, walking along a busy street, when you suddenly 'see' the person who has died. Some people even find themselves following a familiar-looking person to get a closer look so that they can reassure themselves it is not the person they are missing. This is all normal and healthy — part of the process — and not an indication of impending madness. Keep these experiences to yourself unless you have a trusted relative or friend who can listen with compassion and without judgement.

Self-help

Reading this book can be an important step in self-help, as is, somewhat ironically, allowing yourself to accept help from others. It is difficult for most of us to travel this difficult path alone and all help, compassionately given, can enhance our ability to build a new life around the pain of grief.

What else can we do for ourselves? Express whatever we need to, but only show the most vulnerable part of ourselves to those we trust not to judge or to exploit our vulnerability. Keeping a journal can help some — a diary of thoughts and feelings that can give us feedback about our own progress. Use whatever form of expression is familiar to you — an expression of who you are. For example, painting, gardening, walking, working, cooking, playing sport, going to the gym, doing yoga.

We need to make sure we don't get overtired, because we regress at those times and can easily feel overwhelmed. We need just enough tiredness to make sleep easier. We also need to eat well — simple, healthy food — and to have consistent, gentle exercise (or more physically demanding if that is your nature) that ensures that we are breathing properly and using adrenalin. We need sunlight — ten minutes each day if possible of sunlight touching our eyelids because this changes our biochemistry and helps to prevent sadness becoming depression.

We also need to build in change — simple changes on a daily, weekly or monthly basis, that prevent us from slipping into a rut. Change might be as simple as finding a new route to work, school, wherever — one that doesn't bring back too many painful memories. Perhaps doing something nice for yourself on the way home. As well as change, we need to build in simple things to look forward to at the end of each day, week, month.

You can also ask yourself 'What would X (the person who has died) do for me now, or say, if they could see how I am feeling?' The answer to that question might provide some valuable guidelines about what you need right now, and how to take care of that need.

Self-indulgence

Self-indulgence might include some or all of the things already mentioned, like sunlight for instance. Sunlight not only changes our biochemistry, but feels warm and soothing on our skin — almost like the warmth of a hug. Have a nurturing massage. Self-indulgence doesn't have to be expensive or time consuming, but rather a simple reminder that you are important. Buy something new to wear, or indulge your senses — sight, sound, touch, taste, smell. Find something beautiful, stimulating or soothing to look at; use a new perfume, aftershave or shampoo; watch a movie or TV show; listen to sounds that don't plunge you into pits of despair; try something different to cook or eat; and touch something that feels sensuous. You don't have to wait until you feel like doing any of these things for them to be effective — just do them and the effect will eventually follow.

Diet

We have already mentioned the importance of a healthy diet. Appetite for most people decreases in the early days after bereavement or shock, and tastes may change. Grazing is usually better than trying to eat a full meal — grazing on things like fruit, yoghurt, cereal, soup and salad. Avoid anything that is overly spicy, fatty or generally hard to digest. Friends can help by stocking cupboards with fruit and vegetables, eggs, milk, cheese and wholegrain bread. Perhaps they could cook a few simple meals that can be frozen for later use. A multi-vitamin capsule can also be a good idea too, until normal eating is restored.

Memorialisation

Remembering our loved ones

Memorials in a variety of forms have been created throughout social history to acknowledge significant events and honour the lives of people who have died. Memorialisation is a process, usually beginning with a ritual or ceremony, and each culture has its own examples. These rites of passage or markers of transition provide opportunities to acknowledge the meaning and end of a life, and, for many cultures and religions, provide a send-off to the next one.

More lasting memorials are usually created at the end of a relatively long process, which may begin with ritual and ceremony and culminate in a tangible marker. These markers may take the form of a statue, carving, building, geographical site and so on. The pyramids in Egypt and the Taj Mahal in

India are fine examples. Cities, towns and villages sometimes name parks, streets, buildings or rooms in honour of notable citizens who have died. Families and individuals, on the other hand, may choose headstones, jewellery, gardens, paintings, awards, events, orations, books, roadside crosses or political causes for the same purpose.

These days, some people choose to use social media to create a memorial. Sites such as www.onlinememorials.com.au or www.cnet.com/how-to/how-to-memorialize-someones-facebook-account/ can provide a modern, creative alternative to traditional memorials.

Whatever the choice, memorials are confirmation that although people die, our relationships with them live forever.

Ceremony and interment

The first step for most of us after the death of someone we love is to plan and carry out a funeral service and wake. These provide opportunities for people affected by the death to express thoughts and feelings, to share humorous and/or other significant anecdotes and to show appreciation for the impact the person had on their lives.

The next step involves what the funeral industry calls 'disposition of the body'. We will have made decisions prior to the funeral about burial or cremation and where we want the body of our loved one to be placed after the service. Hopefully, many of us will have had the opportunity to discuss our preferences with family and friends long before the decision is needed. Some people will have avoided or postponed this conversation, as they believe it to be morbid or because superstitious beliefs from childhood make them think that death can magically occur simply by talking about it.

Whatever choice we have made, it is important to most people to place the person's body or ashes somewhere that is in keeping with their wishes or personality and is easily accessed. No matter how we think or feel when acutely bereaved, in the long-term most of us want to be able to visit a site where we can focus on the deceased person — to think about them without unnecessary distractions, to cry, talk or just be — to do whatever feels right at the time.

What are the choices?

A grave with a headstone of some kind is a familiar and appropriate choice for many people. A marker in a memorial garden is another. Scattering ashes is still another choice. Other families decide to divide ashes so that each member can make their own choice about where to keep them. These days, many people place at least some of the ashes in jewellery, vases or other ornaments that can be kept close to the heart of the family.

Roadside memorials are now familiar to most of us. They make it hard to drive past without acknowledging to ourselves or others that 'someone died at this spot and someone cares'. Whatever the marker is, or wherever it is placed, it acknowledges the fact that this person's life mattered.

Public memorials

Most countries have memorial sites or services to mark the anniversary of newsworthy deaths. Anzac Day, the Granville rail disaster, the massacre at Port Arthur, Cyclone Tracey, National Sorry Day, Easter and other religious services as well as the dates of significant fires, floods and accidents are usually noted by the Australian media and may involve significant social rituals. Honouring these dates and the people involved reminds us that life is valued, that death can cause pain and that we are all connected to each other as important parts of a mostly compassionate and caring society.

Sometimes the emphasis we place on remembering newsworthy deaths can touch a raw nerve, not only for those most affected by the event, but also for people whose loved one's death only receives recognition from those closest to them. Their reaction might be the question 'Does death have to be dramatic to count?' For a small number of people in many societies, there is no one to care that they have lived or died — surely this is the ultimate sadness. We all want to believe that our own life has been worthwhile and that we and those we love will be remembered, loved and appreciated in some everlasting way.

Memorialisation deserves thoughtful consideration. The ways we currently choose to honour and memorialise our fellow citizens, family members, colleagues, friends and neighbours will be as revealing to historians, anthropologists and sociologists in the future as it is now to our young children. Memorials don't have to be elaborate, expensive or visible to the wider community — whatever form they take, they are indicators of the value we place on relationships.

Writing – journal,
email or letters

We have already mentioned journal writing or keeping a diary, but writing is worth mentioning again. Don't allow yourself to be pressured into writing because someone else thinks it is a good idea — it only has benefit if writing is something you do naturally. One of its benefits is that it can become an invaluable support in the middle of the night when sleep eludes you and friends are unavailable. It is at these times that you can pour out thoughts and feelings in a journal, letter or an email to an understanding friend or relative, using writing as a kind of emotional 'chuck bowl'. Worries, concerns, lists of tasks can also be put on paper in the middle of the night so that they don't remain inside, cluttering an already overloaded system.

Distraction

Learning to live with grief is largely about the 'art of distraction'. Whenever we are experiencing emotional pain, it is helpful to stay with it long enough to understand its source, express whatever we need to in whatever way feels right, then distract ourselves by doing something physical that restores normal breathing. Choose an activity that would normally give you pleasure — something that draws attention into the external world, away from the dark emptiness and loneliness of the internal world.

Bereavement counselling

Counselling can be invaluable for people of all ages — from about three years onwards. Not everybody needs to have counselling, but we all need access to what good counselling can provide. That is, the listening ear of someone who is wise, compassionate, loving and ethical. If friends with these qualities are not available, or we fear overloading others and fear they may begin to avoid us because we seem too needy, contacting a trained professional is a good idea. Some people provide their services on a voluntary basis — for example, through churches, government agencies and so on — but the majority charge a fee.

Bereavement counselling does not mean being locked into seeing someone weekly, or several times weekly as may be the case with certain forms of psychotherapy. Sessions may initially be spaced twice weekly, then three or so, with the spaces gradually increasing as need decreases. Spacing is determined by individual need, financial constraints, and the counsellor's availability. The 'contract' is usually open-ended, meaning that counselling doesn't come to a sudden stop, but later allows for quite long spaces between sessions, always with the possibility of resuming contact whenever life events impact on grief. Some counsellors provide email access and support between sessions, or on occasions, instead of face-to-face sessions.

The number of sessions can range from a one-off — usually for those who are doing OK in the circumstances and just need reassurance, plus a few additional strategies to manage their grief — to forty or so, over a period of five to six years. Parents grieving the loss of very young children, particularly those who die suddenly, and those who are older and lonely with little or no family support, tend to have more sessions and for a longer period. Counsellors do not usually stay around until bereaved people are happy again, but they will hopefully be available until it is clear that the bereaved person has the ability to build life around their loss.

Conclusion

The impact of grief

Repetitive themes in this book — for the bereaved — have been around the impact of grief on all levels of being, the importance of expressing whatever is necessary and not being restricted by the needs of others, the need for wise, compassionate and non-judgemental support, and the length of time it takes to rebuild a shattered world.

For helpers, themes have been around making the situation safe, supporting without judgement or the tendency to restrict the behaviour of grieving people because of their own discomfort, providing practical help, and doing things with the bereaved person. Don't avoid them for fear of upsetting them — they *are* upset, but you can give them an invaluable opportunity to express their upset.

Your presence and comfort are important. Don't say things like 'If there is anything I can do to help, let me know', because bereaved people usually don't have the ability to ask for help. Just do it. Churches, neighbourhood groups and colleagues are often very willing to help once they know how, and it usually takes simply one person to take charge, decide on an idea or organise a roster, and co-opt others to help. Grief is something we will all experience, not a 'them and us' situation. It is not contagious.

As a community we are affected by whatever happens to others in that community. We have a responsibility to help each other in need, just as we have to rejoice in the good things that happen. If we join together in times of crisis, we make most things survivable and enhance the quality of life for everyone.

Community education

The subject of death is often taboo. The very mention of the word can trigger regression and, from that very young perspective, we tend to become superstitious, consciously believing or unconsciously fearing that if we talk about it, we can make *it* happen. Our fears can make us avoid people who need our help, even avoid doing something sensible like making a will. When possible, organise a discussion group in your local setting (with willing people) so that the topic can be addressed and discussed in safety. The following suggestions may give you some ideas about how to begin.

Discussion starters (community education settings or discussion groups)

The American psychiatrist Robert Jay Lifton says, 'It is important to talk about death because death is so integral to life… Suppressing our relationship with death is a form of numbing which spreads to other areas and tends to limit our capacity for feeling in general, or our vitality.'

Q1: What was Lifton attempting to say in this quote? Do you agree with him?

Some other possible questions:

Q2: What if death took a holiday, and everyone lived forever? What would happen (a) environmentally, and (b) to relationships?

Q3: Would you like to know the exact time you will die? Why, or why not?

Q4: If someone you cared for had three months to a year to live, how might you treat them differently?

Q5: Do you think that some deaths are worse than others? What makes them worse? Would your response to a bereaved person be different if they were grieving from one of those 'worse' deaths?

Q6: It is sometimes said that quality of life is more important than quantity. What do we mean by 'quality of life'?

Q7: What do you fear most about death — the process of dying, the unknown, or concern for the suffering of those you would leave behind?

Q8: How would you like to be remembered? What would you like your epitaph to be?

Q9: Would you like to be buried or cremated? What influenced your choice?

Q10: Would you like to be an organ donor? Which organs would you like to donate? Not donate? What would influence your decision? Have you discussed the pros and cons of donations with your family?

Other suggestions

Some groups may find it helpful to visit a chapel, crematorium or cemetery together at a time when no one is raw with grief. Reactions can be explored later or occasionally during the 'field visit'. Visits like this, including with children, can be valuable in reducing fear, and in increasing people's ability to make informed choices when needed.

Counselling resources

Australian Centre for Grief and Bereavement

McCulloch House, Monash Medical Centre
246 Clayton Road, Clayton, Victoria 3168
www.grief.org.au
Phone: 1800 642 066
Email: info@grief.org.au

Bereavement C.A.R.E. Centre

14 Hollis Avenue, Eastwood, NSW 2122
PO Box 327, Epping, NSW 1710
Phone: 1300 654 556
www.bereavementcare.com.au
Email: info@bereavementcare.com.au

CanTeen
Level 11, 130 Elizabeth Street, Sydney, NSW 2000
GPO Box 3821 Sydney, NSW 2001
www.canteen.org.au
Phone: 1800 226 833
Email: admin@canteen.org.au

Community Health Centres — all states

The Compassionate Friends
4th Floor, Room 404, 32 York Street
    Sydney, NSW 2000
www.thecompassionatefriends.org.au
Phone: (02) 9290 2355
info@tcfnsw.org.au
(Check phone book for address and phone number in
other states)

Good Grief (Mary MacKillop Centre)
Level 3, 12 Mount Street, North Sydney, NSW 2060
PO Box 1023, North Sydney, NSW 2059
www.goodgrief.org.au
Phone: (02) 8912 2700
Email: info@goodgrief.org.au

Homicide Victims' Support Group (HVSG)–NSW
Level 1a, 239 Church Street, Parramatta, NSW 2150
http://hvsgnsw.org.au
Phone: 1800 191 777
Email: info@hvsgnsw.org.au

Lifeline
All states — 131 114

Marriage and Family Counselling Centres — all states

National Association for Loss and Grief
(02) 9489 6644 — branches in all states

The National Centre for Childhood Grief
('A Friend's Place')
PO Box 327, Epping, NSW 1710
www.childhoodgrief.org.au
Phone: 1300 654 556
Email: info@childhoodgrief.org.au
Outreach email: afriendsplace@me.org.au

SIDS & Kids
www.sidsandkids.org
Phone: 1300 308 307

Memorialisation websites
www.onlinememorials.com.au
www.cnet.com/how-to/how-to-memorialize-someones-facebook-account/

Further reading

For a list of books appropriate to your needs, contact:

Open Leaves
www.openleaves.com.au
1/109 Gladstone Road, Highgate Hill, QLD 4101

Compassion Books USA
www.compassionbooks.com
A few helpful titles:

Thomas Attig, *How We Grieve: Relearning the World*, Oxford University Press, NY 1996.

Kenneth J. Doka (ed.), *Living with Grief After Sudden Loss*, Hospice Foundation of America, 1996.

Janice Harris Lord, *No Time for Goodbyes*, Millenium Books, Newtown, NSW, 1988.

Ann McDonald, *Softly My Grief*, McPhee Gribble/Penguin, Melbourne, 1988.

Harriet Schiff, *The Bereaved Parent*, Penguin, Melbourne, 1978.

About the Authors

Mal and Dianne McKissock established the Bereavement C.A.R.E. Centre in 1981, originally in Randwick, moving later to Lewisham, then Epping and later Eastwood. In 1994, they founded the National Centre for Childhood Grief, now known as 'A Friend's Place', and were clinical directors of both services until their retirement in January 2015.

Patrons of 'A Friend's Place', they remain closely connected to all of the Centre's services in an advisory capacity and continue to teach in some of its training courses.

Mal and Dianne have taught widely in Australia and many other countries, and have published many books and articles on the subject of grief and bereavement. They are both members of the International Work Group on Death, Dying and Bereavement, and in 1996 were awarded the Order of Australia Medal for their services to the bereaved community.

They currently live on the Central Coast of New South Wales and can be contacted via email: mmckissock@icloud.com and dmckissock@icloud.com

As part of the outreach service of the NCCG, Dianne continues to provide an email support service for dying and bereaved people of all ages and for those involved in their care.